awakening wisdom

The Buddha

Michael S. Russo

D1570915

SophiaOmni

ISBN: 978-1539858737

SophiaOmni

Visit our website at:
www.sophiaomni.org

Contents

Meditating Buddha (Sarnath, India, 5th century)

Preface

About 2,600 years ago, a young nobleman named Siddhattha Gotama left his family's home in Southern Nepal and
set out on the quest for liberation. One night while sitting
under the mythic Bodhi tree, he had a profound and life-changing
experience that awakened him. He became "the Buddha."

The way of life that the Buddha espoused caught on rather
quickly. By the time he died at the age of 80, Buddhist monasteries could be found throughout India, and, within several centuries
of his death, Buddhism would spread throughout Asia, becoming
the dominant "religion" of that continent.

More recently the teachings of the Buddha have made inroads
in the West—particularly in the United States—with the pioneer-
ing work of people like Alan Watts, D.T. Suzuki, and Beat writers
such as Alan Gingsberg and Jack Kerouac. Today, in your own
neighborhood or not very far away from it, there is probably at
least one Buddhist community meeting regularly and offering
some form of meditation. Around the country Buddhist mindfulness practice—or at least a popular spin on it—is now being
taught in schools, prisons, hospitals, and even at corporate head-
quarters and military bases.

What accounts for the popularity of Buddhism in the United States? At a time when many Americans—and particularly
younger Americans—are moving from traditional forms of orga-
nized religion, there is still a hunger to discover deeper spiritual
and moral practices that can reduce the suffering that is an inevitable part of life. We may not want to have authority figures
telling us how to behave or what to think, but that doesn't mean
that we don't want the kind of structure and support that religious

communities traditionally have provided.

And this is where the Buddha comes in.

The methods that the Buddha developed thousands of years ago as a means of relieving his own suffering and the suffering of all beings is as relevant today as when he first taught. The Buddha's approach is skeptical, non-dogmatic, pragmatic, and completely rationalistic—a perfect fit for Americans living in the 21st century.

The problem is that what often passes for the actual thought of the historic Buddha himself is typically more of a reflection of the way Buddhism has manifested itself in various cultures around the world than it is a true representation of his own radical and groundbreaking thought. The Buddha, for example, never thought of himself as a God, or as someone to be worshipped, but if you go to Buddhist temples around the world, that's exactly what's being emphasized.

Unfortunately, many people who refer to themselves as "Buddhists" may never have actually read the teachings of the Buddha as they were passed down in the Pali Cannon. There's a simple reason for this: The Pali Cannon is a massive work that evolved though through centuries of oral tradition and is filled with archaic language as well as tons of frustrating repetitions. Whereas you can probably carry the Bible or the Koran under your arm, if you tried to transport all of the volumes of the Pali Canon this way, you'd soon develop serious back problems.

What I've attempted to do in this small volume called *Awakening Wisdom* is to try to share the earliest teachings of Buddhism by using carefully selected and judiciously edited texts from the Pali Canon. While recognizing that the texts of the Pali Canon already represent embellishments on the thought of the Buddha, this is the closest that we can get to his actual thought. For better or for worse, if we're ever going to discover what the Buddha actually taught to his monks in Northern India so long ago, this is where we have to start.

My approach in translating and updating discourses from the Pali Canon was to aim at readability rather than trying to achieve scholarly exactitude. This text is written primarily for novices to the field of Buddhism, but also for practicing Buddhists who may never have encountered the seminal texts of the Pali Canon before. Because the Pali Canon is written in—you guessed it!—Pali, I've opted to stick with the less common Pali terminology rather than the more common Sanskrit (e.g., *"Nibbāna"* and *"kamma"* rather than *"Nirvāna"* and *"karma."*). A short glossary of Pali terminology has been included in the back if you get confused by any of the terms used in this text.

The title of this book should serve as an indication of its two-fold aim: The "awakening" in *Awakening Wisdom* is both an adjective and a gerund. In the first sense, the goal is to illuminate the wisdom taught by the Buddha that leads to awakening by focusing specifically on the ideas presented in the Pali Canon.

But in its more active sense, the title indicates that a book like this is not simply meant as a kind of intellectual archeology. The Buddha's wisdom is meant to be lived out in our daily lives. Scores of men and women throughout the centuries have benefitted from this wisdom and as a result have attained various degrees of liberation from their suffering. A few—and you could be part of this illustrious crowd—have attained the kind of awakening that the Buddha assured us was possible for all. So Buddhism is not just about understanding ideas…as important as proper understanding may be. It's also about developing specific practices that can make your life more harmonious and peaceful right here and now.

A work like this one wouldn't be possible without the assistance of many individuals. My sincerest thanks, therefore, go out to Donald Cornelius, Joseph Schifilliti, JoAnn Miller, Rayaz Khan and Marie Dollard who offered numerous suggestions on parts of this text as well as to the teachers and members of the Inisfada Zendo on Long Island for constantly providing me with dynamic examples of Buddhism in action.

Buddha Gallery (Wat Chaimongkhon, Ayutthaya, Thiland, 14th century)

CHAPTER I

Siddhattha

The 6th century BCE, the period during which the Buddha lived, was a time of great social and political change in India. New kingdoms were being established throughout India, cities were increasing in size, and an expansion in trade led to the creation of a more affluent society with a thriving merchant class. Tremendous change was occurring as well at this time in the realm of spiritual thought. The ritualistic emphasis described in the *Vedas* was being supplanted in some circles by the more mystical approach of the *Upanishads*. This led to a dramatic increase in the number of men opting for the radical life of wandering ascetics—those who rejected the materialistic lifestyle found in the towns and cities in pursuit of spiritual liberation.

The person that we refer to as the Buddha was born Siddhattha Gotama (Sanskrit: Siddhartha Gautama). Unfortunately, the date of the Buddha's birth and the basic facts of his life are subject to dispute by scholars. The traditional dates of the Buddha's life are generally given as 566-486 BCE, although some scholars today argue that he may have lived as much as a century later (possibly from about 490-410 BCE). The oldest source that we have from the Pali Canon offers only scattered bibliographical information and the accuracy of even some of these accounts is subject to doubt. Indeed, many of the "facts" that we have about the Buddha's life are derived from later devotional works like the *Buddhacarita* of Aśvaghosa, composed centuries after the Buddha's death and of questionable historical value. Despite the scarcity of reliable sources, there are basic biographical details about the

Buddha that have now become part of the common narrative of his life.

Early Life

According to traditional accounts, Siddhattha was said to have been born in Kapilavastu in what is today Southern Nepal around 566 BC as a nobleman in the Gotama family of the the Sakya clan. The name Siddhartha literally means "he who has achieved his goal." He is also referred to in later Buddhist literature as "Shakyamuni" or "the sage of the Sakya clan." Siddhartha's father, Suddhodana, is often described as a king, but in greater likelihood was probably the leading nobleman of Kapilavastu, where his family lived. While not a member of royalty himself, the aristocratic background of the Buddha would have opened up many doors for him at courts in Northern India later in life when he began his career as a spiritual teacher.

Legend tells that when Siddhattha was conceived, his mother Maya dreamed that a white elephant had entered her womb. When she was about to give birth, Maya travelled, as was customary, from Kapilavastu to deliver her child at her family's home. Stopping at a garden in Lumbini, she gave birth to him standing up in the shade of a Sal tree. Seven days after his birth, the Buddha's mother died. Suddhodana would later remarry and his new wife, Mahapajapati, would raise Siddhartha and his half-brother, Nanda.

After Siddhattha was born, his father summoned fortune tellers to predict the boy's future and was told that, if he remained in the world, he would become the powerful king of a unified India; but, if he abandoned the world, he would instead become a great spiritual leader. Suddhodana, not surprisingly, preferred the former path and decided to surround his son with every luxury imaginable, keeping him away from the kinds of unpleasantries in life that at the time were thought to compel people to enter the spiritual life. As Siddhattha himself describes his early life:

...I was delicately nurtured, most delicately nurtured, extremely delicately nurtured. At my father's residence lotus ponds were made just for my enjoyment: in one of them blue lotuses blossomed, in another red lotuses, and in a third white lotuses....By day and night a white canopy was held over me so that cold and heat, dust, grass, and dew would not settle on me. I had three mansions: one for winter, one for summer, and one for the rainy season. I spent the four months of the rainy season...being entertained by musicians, none of whom were male, and I did not leave the mansion. (AN 1.145, p. 139-140)

At the age of sixteen Siddhattha married a young noblewoman named Yasodhara, and had a son with her who was named Rahula. His son's name literally means "fetter" or "obstacle," which may indicate that, even as a young man, Siddhartha may have felt a certain amount of ambivalence about the life that was chosen for him by his father. There must have been a tension between the desire to remain in his father's household—with all the pleasures and luxuries that this life afforded him—and the desire to explore the contemplative life and possibly attain liberation.

The Four Sights

As he approached his 30th birthday, one day Siddhattha persuaded his charioteer, Channa, to take him beyond the palace walls. While on this ride, he encountered a withered old man for the first time. Asking Channa what was wrong with the man, he was told that debilitating old age was the destiny of all human beings. Returning to the palace, Siddhattha was filled with uneasiness and was incapable of finding pleasure in his luxurious surroundings. On a second ride outside the palace, he encountered a very sick man, lying on the side of the road. On a third, he saw a corpse. Exposed to the reality of the human condition, Siddhattha realized for the first time that no amount of pleasure could provide one with ultimate happiness in a world filled with sickness, suffering, old age, and ultimately death.

Finally, on a fourth trip outside the palace, he encountered a wandering ascetic of the type that was undoubtedly common in northern India at the time, sitting under a tree engaged in deep meditation. When he inquired about this individual, his charioteer informed him that the ascetic had abandoned the world to seek liberation from suffering. Inspired by the possibility of attaining liberation himself, Siddhattha immediately resolved to adopt this same way of life.

And so, in the middle of the night, while his family was still sleeping, Siddhattha left the palace, shaved his head, and began the life of a renunciate. "Later, while still young…endowed with the blessing of youth…," he recalled, "though my mother and father wished otherwise and wept with tearful faces, I shaved off my hair and beard, put on the yellow robe, and went forth from home-life into homelessness." (MN 26.14, p. 256). His ultimate goal in leaving home and family, as he himself would later put it, was to seek the "unaging, unailing, deathless, sorrowless, and undefiled supreme security from bondage, *Nibbāna*" (MN 26.13, p. 256).

What is evident from the story of the four sights—which is probably not literally true—is that it tells us that from an age when most people are content to focus on material pleasure, Siddhattha was already a deeply introspective individual, who probably suffered from no small amount of existential anxiety. "This world, alas, is in a sorry state," he somberly reflected to himself. "There is birth and decay….And no one knows any way of escape from this suffering….When will deliverance be found from this suffering, this aging and death?" (DN 14.2.18, p. 211) Although he had the opportunity to live out his life as a respected leader of the Sakya clan, like most great visionaries throughout human history, Siddhattha refused simply to accept the status quo and was willing to sacrifice everything that ordinary people think so important to realize ultimate liberation from suffering.

READING THE SOURCES

---~~~---

The Four Sites
[Mahapadana Sutta]

After much time had passed, the young lord Gotama told his charioteer, "Harness the state carriages, charioteer, and we will go to inspect the pleasure park."...Then Gotama mounted a state carriage and drove in procession to the park.

As he was driving past the park, the young lord saw an aged man as bent as a roof beam, decrepit, leaning on a staff, tottering as he walked, afflicted and long past his prime. And seeing him Gotama said: "What is wrong with that man, charioteer? His hair and body are not like that of other men?"

"He is what is called an old man, my lord."

"But why is he called an old man?"

"He is called old, my lord, because he has not much longer to live."

"But then am I liable to become old and not exempt from old age?"

"Both you and I, my lord, are liable to become old and not exempt from old age."

"That's enough of the park for today, charioteer. Drive me back now to the palace."

"Yes, my lord," answered the charioteer, and drove him back. And he, going to his rooms, sat brooding sorrowful and depressed, thinking, "Shame then on this thing called birth, since he who is born must eventually become old!"

E. H. Brewster, ed. *The Life of Gotama the Buddha.* London: Kegan Paul, Trench, Trubner, and Co., 1926. Translation updated. Alt Trans: DN 14. 2.1-2.18, pp. 207-211.

Thereupon the king sent for the charioteer and asked him: "Well, did the young lord take pleasure in the park? Was he pleased with it?"

"No, my lord, he was not."

"What then did he see on his drive?"

And the charioteer told the king all.

Then the king thought: "We must not have Gotama declining to rule. We must not have him going forth from the house into the homeless state. We must not let what the brahman soothsayers foretold come true." So, that these things might not come to pass, he let the youth be still more surrounded by sensuous pleasures. And thus Gotama continued to live amidst the pleasures of sense.

After much time had passed by, the young lord commanded his charioteer to drive him to the pleasure park as before.

And, as he was driving to the park, Gotama saw, a sick man, suffering and very ill, fallen in his own urine, by some being lifted up and by others being dressed. Seeing this, Gotama asked: "What has happened to that man? His eyes are not like others' eyes, nor his head like the head of other men?"

"He is what is called a sick man, my lord."

"But why is he called a sick man?"

"He is called so, my lord, because he can hardly recover from his illness."

"But I am also then liable to become sick and not exempt from sickness?"

"Both you and I, my lord, are liable to become sick and are not exempt from sickness."

"That's enough of the park for today, charioteer. Drive me back to the palace."

"Yes, my lord," answered the charioteer, and drove him back.

And, going to his rooms, he sat brooding sorrowful and depressed, thinking, "Shame then on this thing called birth, since he who is born must experience sickness."

Thereupon the king sent for the charioteer and asked him: "Well, did the young lord take pleasure in the park and was he pleased with it?"

"No, my lord, he was not."

"What did he see then on his drive?"

And the charioteer told the king all.

Then the king thought: "We must not have Gotama declining

to rule; we must not have him going forth from the house to the homeless state; we must not let what the brahman soothsayers spoke of come true." So, that these things might not come to pass, he let the young man be still more abundantly surrounded by sensuous pleasures. And thus Gotama continued to live amidst the pleasures of sense.

After much time had passed, the young lord Gotama once again commanded his charioteer to drive him to the park.

As he was driving to the park, he saw a great crowd of people clad in garments of different colors constructing a funeral pyre. And seeing this he asked his charioteer: "Why now are all those people come together in garments of different colors, and making that pyre?"

"It is because someone, my lord, has died."

"Then drive the carriage over to where the dead man is."

"Yes, my lord," answered the charioteer, and did so. And Gotama saw the corpse of the dead man and asked: "Why is he called a dead man?"

"It means, my lord, that neither his parents nor his other relatives will ever see him again, nor will he see them."

"But am I also then subject to death, not exempt from dying?"

"Both you and I, my lord, are subject to death, not exempt from dying."

"That's enough of the park for today, charioteer. Drive me back to the palace."

"Yes, my lord," replied the charioteer, and drove him back.

And, going into his rooms, he sat brooding sorrowful and depressed, thinking: "Shame upon this thing called birth, since he who is born must experience death."

As before, the king questioned the charioteer who told him what happened, and the king let Gotama be surrounded by even more sensuous enjoyment. And thus he continued to live amidst the pleasures of sense.

After much time had passed by, the Lord Gotama commanded his charioteer once again to drive him to the pleasure park.

And, as he was driving to the park he saw a shaven-headed man, a recluse, wearing the yellow robe. And seeing him he asked the charioteer, "What is the matter with that man? His head is unlike other men's heads and his clothes too are unlike those of others."

"That is what they call a recluse, because, my lord, he is one who has gone forth."

"What does it mean, 'to have gone forth'?"

"To have gone forth, my lord, means being thorough in the religious life, thorough in the peaceful life, thorough in good action, thorough in meritorious conduct, thorough in harmlessness, thorough in kindness to all creatures."

"Excellent indeed is what they call a recluse, since his conduct is so thorough in all respects. Drive the carriage over to that man."

"Yes, my lord," replied the charioteer and drove up to the recluse. Then Gotama addressed him, saying, "Master, what have you done that your head is not as other men's heads, nor your clothes as those of other men?"

"I, my lord, am one whose has gone forth."

"What, master, does that mean?"

"It means, my lord, being thorough in the religious life, thorough in the peaceful life, thorough in good actions, thorough in meritorious conduct, thorough in harmlessness, thorough in kindness to all creatures."

"Excellently indeed, master, are you said to have gone forth, since so thorough is your conduct in all those respects." Then the lord Gotama said to his charioteer: "You take the carriage and drive it back to the palace. But I will stay here and cut off my hair, put on the yellow robe, and go forth from the house into the homeless state."

"Yes, my lord," replied the charioteer, and drove back to the palace. And the prince Gotama there and then cutting off his hair and putting on the yellow robe, went forth from the house into the homeless state.

Now at Kapilavatthu, the kings's seat, some eighty-four thousand people heard of what prince Gotama had done and thought: "Surely this is no common teaching, this is no common going forth, for prince Gotama has shaved his head and has put on the yellow robe and has gone forth from the house into the homeless state. If prince Gotama has done this, why shouldn't we as well?" And they all had their heads shaved and put on the yellow robes, and in imitation of the Bodhisatta they went forth into the homeless state. So the Bodhisatta went up on his rounds through the villages, towns and cities accompanied by that multitude.

Now when he was meditating in seclusion, Gotama the Bodhi-satta had this thought: "It is not suitable for me to live with a crowd like this. It would be better if I were to live alone, far from the crowd." So after a time he left the crowd and lived alone. Those eighty-four thousand recluses went one way, and the Bodhisatta went another way.

When Gotama the Bodhisatta had gone to his dwelling and was meditating alone, he thought: "Truly the world is in a troubled state—there is birth and decay, there is death, there is falling from one state and springing up in another. O when shall deliverance be found from this suffering, decay, and death?"

Seeking Awakening
[Ariyapariyesana Sutta]

Monks, before my awakening.., I, being subject to birth, sought out what was also subject to birth; being subject to aging, I sought out what was also subject to aging; being subject to sickness....death...sorrow...[and] defilement, I sought out what was also subject to sickness...death...sorrow... [and] defilement.

Then, monks, I thought to myself, "Why do I, being subject to birth...aging...sickness...death...sorrow...[and] defilement, seek out what was also subject to birth...aging...sickness... death...sorrow...[and] defilement?"

What if I, being subject to birth, having grasped the danger in what is subject to birth, instead sought out the birthless, supreme security of *Nibbāna*? What if I, being subject to aging... sickness...death...sorrow...[and] defilement, having grasped the danger in what is subject to aging...sickness...death...sorrow... [and] defilement, instead sought out the ageless, sickless, deathless, sorrowless, undefiled, supreme security of *Nibbāna*?

Then...while I was still a young man with black hair, in possession of the blessings of youth and still in the prime of my life,

---

Alt Trans: MN 26.13-14, p. 256.

though my parents were opposed to it and wept tearfully, I shaved off my hair and beard. And putting on the yellow robes went forth from home into the homeless life.

CHAPTER II

Becoming the Buddha

In an attempt to discover the path to liberation, Siddhattha went to study with two prominent teachers of meditation—Arada Kelama and Udraka Ramaputra. Under the guidance of these teachers, Siddhattha was said to have reached the highest states of meditative absorption that their methods were able to offer, but in the end both failed to provide him with ultimate liberation. "This [teaching]," he informed his teachers, "does not lead to disenchantment, to dispassion, to cessation, to peace, to direct knowledge, to enlightenment, to *Nibbāna*...." (MN 26.16, p. 259).

Later on he met up with a group of five ascetics and took up their way of life, practicing extreme self-mortification for several years. The aim of this sort of radical ascetic practice, which was also common in the Brahmanical tradition at the time, was to subdue the body to such a degree that the passions that were thought to lead human beings astray could be subdued. At one point it is written that he lived on the most minimal amount of food possible—the legendary one grain of rice a day. Not surprisingly, his physical health began to suffer as a result:

> Because of eating so little my limbs became like the jointed segments of vine stems or bamboo stems. Because of eating so little my backside became like a camel's hoof. Because of eating so little the projections on my spine stood forth like corded beads. Because of eating so little my ribs jutted out as gaunt as the crazy rafters of an old roofless barn. Because of eating so little the gleam of my eyes sank far down in their sockets, looking like the gleam of water

that has sunk far down in a deep well. Because of eating so little my scalp shriveled and withered as a green bitter gourd shrivels and withers in the wind and sun. Because of eating so little my belly skin adhered to my backbone; thus if I touched my belly skin I encountered my backbone and if I touched my backbone I encountered my belly skin. Because of eating so little, if I defecated or urinated, I fell over on my face there. Because of eating so little, if I tried to ease my body by rubbing my limbs with my hands, the hair, rotted at its roots, fell from my body as I rubbed (MN 36.28, p. 339).

Eventually he realized that this type of radical asceticism would not lead to liberation, and if continued would almost certainly cause him to die.

One day, according to legend, he was offered a meal of boiled rice and porridge by a girl and ate it (MN 36.33). With this he recognized the insight of the "middle way"—the recognition that neither the extremes of hedonism nor of asceticism ultimately led to liberation:

[T]hese two extremes should not be followed by one who has gone forth into homelessness. What two? The pursuit of sensual happiness in sensual pleasures, which is low, vulgar, the way of worldlings, ignoble, unbeneficial; and the pursuit of self-mortification, which is painful, ignoble, unbeneficial. Without veering towards either of these extremes, the *Tathagata* has awakened to the middle way, which gives rise to vision, which gives rise to knowledge, which leads to peace, to enlightenment..." (SN 56.11, p. 1844).

Awakening

When his five ascetic companions saw that he had abandoned the ascetic path, they left him in disgust. Siddhattha, however, realized that he was on the right track, and so he resolved to sit under a large tree (later to be called a Bodhi tree in his honor) near the town of Bodhgaya until he became awakened or died. He spent three nights under the tree in perfect stillness, and on the third night had an awakening experience—an immediate insight into the nature of reality that left him profoundly, and by all accounts, permanently transformed. At that moment he became the Buddha. The Sanskrit root *budh* means "to wake up," so the name Buddha literally means "the awakened one."

This title is an apt one indeed, because unlike the founders of other major religions of the world, the Buddha never made any claims to divinity. It is said that not long after his experience under the Bodhi tree, the Buddha passed a stranger on the road who was so taken by his calm demeanor that he asked, "Are you a god?" The Buddha replied, "No, I am not." Then what are you?" the stranger inquired. "I am awake," he said. (SN 4.36, pp. 425-426). The point of this story is that the Buddha never sought to present himself as anything other than a flesh and blood human being. What he had attained in his life, any of us can also attain by following the same path that he did.

Siddhattha's experience was undoubtedly profound, but he was worried that human beings with their worldly preoccupations could never begin to understand the depths of what he experienced while sitting in meditation under the Bodhi tree:

> [How can I try to teach] what I found with so much hardship? This [teaching] is not easily understood by those oppressed by lust and hate. Those fired by lust, obscured by darkness, will never see this abstruse [teaching], deep, hard to see, subtle, going against the stream" (SN 1.6.1, pp. 231-232).

Although at first Siddhattha was hesitant to try to explain to others the truth that he had discovered, he decided that he needed to share his insights out of compassion for mankind. Leaving Bodhgaya, he travelled 130 miles north to Sarnath, near the ancient city of Benares (Varanasi), where his five former companions had gone. After some initial hesitation, he was welcomed by his former associates, who were perceptive enough to recognize the profound change that had occurred in him. There in the Deer Park at Sarnath, he preached his first sermon, called "Setting in Motion the Wheel of the Dhamma," in which he shared what has become known as the Four Noble Truths and the Eightfold Path (SN 56.11, p. 1843-147).

Public Ministry of the Buddha

At the age of 35 the Buddha—as we will now refer to him—began his public ministry, spreading his teachings (Pali: *dhamma*; San: *dharma)* throughout Northern India. His five companions formed the foundation of a new order of *bhikkhus* (San: *bhiksu*) or monks—considered by some scholars to be the oldest historical institution on the planet (Smith and Novak, 12). This new order is referred to as the *sangha* or community and originally was comprised specifically of ordained monks who followed the teachings of the Buddha, although today the term is used to refer to any Buddhist community. These three elements—the Buddha, the *dhamma*, and the *sangha*—which are referred to in Buddhism as "The Three Refuges," have become the three foundations of religious life for all Buddhists.

Because of his own charisma and the depth of his teachings, the Buddha soon began to attract numerous followers. One of these, the wealthy merchant Sudatta, was so taken by the Buddha's teachings that he donated land in Sravasti to the sangha in the Jeta Grove and built the Jeta Monastery. This became a central location for Buddhist monks to gather during the rainy season, when travel in India became difficult.

As the *dhamma* spread throughout northern India, the Buddha began to attract female lay followers to his teachings. Five years after his enlightenment, the Buddha received his stepmother Mahapajapati, who came to visit him with a large group of women. She requested that they be permitted to join the monastic order. Initially, the Buddha refused this request, but eventually he relented, establishing an order of *bhikkhuni* (San: *bhiksuni*) or nuns.

READING THE SOURCES

—∽∿∽—

The Noble Quest
[Ariyapariyesana Sutta]

The Awakening of the Buddha

Then, monks, still searching for what was good, seeking the incomparable, noble state of peace, I entered Magadha and came to the army town of Uruvela. There I saw a delightful stretch of land, a pleasing forest with a clear, flowing river, and a nearby town suitable for collecting alms.

I thought to myself…, "Certainly, this is a delightful [place]… This is just the right kind of place for the exertions of a young man set on exerting himself." So I sat down right there, monks, thinking, "This place will serve for my exertions."

Then, monks, being myself subject to birth, having grasped the danger in what is subject to birth, while seeking the birthless, supreme security of *Nibbāna*, I attained the birthless, supreme security of *Nibbāna*. Being subject to aging…sickness…death…sorrow…[and] defilement, having grasped the danger in what is subject to aging…sickness…death…sorrow…[and] defilement, while seeking ageless, sickless, deathless, sorrowless, undefiled, supreme security of *Nibbāna*, I attained the ageless, sickless, deathless, sorrowless, undefiled, supreme security of *Nibbāna*. This knowledge and vision arose within me: "My liberation is complete; this is my last birth; there is no longer any becoming-again."

Alt Trans: MN 26.17-18, 25-27, 30, pp. 259-260, 263-266

Then, monks, the thought occurred to me: "This *dhamma* that I have attained is profound, difficult to see and understand, peaceful and deep, beyond the powers of mere reasoning, subtle, and only to be experienced by those possessing wisdom. But this is a generation that delights in pleasure, is devoted to pleasure, and rejoices in pleasure. For [such a generation], it is hard to see this truth—namely, this dependent arising. And it is also hard to see this truth—namely, the quieting of mental activity, the letting go of all attachments, the end of craving, dispassion, cessation, *Nibbāna*.

But, if I were to teach this *dhamma* and others did not understand me, that would be tiring for me and troubling to me...."

This was my state of mind: I was inclined to inaction and not to the teaching of the *dhamma*....

Then Brahma Sahampati, intuiting with his mind the state of my mind...said this to me: "...Arise, conquering hero...and walk without debt through the world. Let the Blessed One teach the *dhamma*. There will be those who will understand."

The Buddha Begins His Ministry

Then the question came to me, "To whom should I teach this *dhamma* first? Who will understand this *dhamma* quickly?"...Then it occurred to me, "The group of five monks who attended me when I first set out striving were very helpful. Why don't I teach the dhamma to them first?" Then I wondered, "Where are these five monks staying now?" And with the divine eye, which, purified, surpasses the human eye, I saw that they were staying near Varanasi in the Deer Park at Isipatana.

Then, after dwelling as long as I wanted at Uruvela, I set out for Varanasi. On the road between Gaya and the place of Awakening, Ajivaka Upaka saw me and said: "My friend, your faculties are clear, your skin is pure and bright. Under whose guidance have you gone forth? Who is your teacher? Whose *dhammas* do you teach?"

When this was said, I replied to Ajivaka Upaka in the following verses:

All-conquering, all knowing am I,
undefiled by things, renouncing all,
freed from all craving.
Knowing all this for myself,
to whom should I point as teacher?

For one like me, there is no teacher,
and none like me can be found.
In this world with all its gods,
there is no one who is my counterpart.

I am the perfect one in the world;
I am the supreme teacher;
I alone am fully self-awakened.
With fires cooled, I am liberated.

To set in motion the *dhamma* wheel,
I go to the city of Kasi.
In a world that has become blind,
I go forth, beating the drum of deathlessness.

[Then Ajivaka Upaka said]: "By your claims, my friend, you seem to declare yourself a universal conquerer."
[And I replied:]

The conquerors are those like me
who have achieved the elimination of defilements.
I have conquered all evil states.
Therefore, Upaka, I am the conqueror.

When this was said, Ajivaka Upaka said, "May it be so, my friend." Then shaking his head, he took a different path and went his way.

The Buddha Seeks Out His Five Companions

Then, monks, wandering along by stages, I arrived at Varanasi, to the Deer Park at Isipatana, where the group of five monks were staying. The five, seeing me approaching in the distance, agreed upon the following with one another: "Here comes Gotama the ascetic. He has been living decadently and has given up his striving, living in luxury. He shouldn't be greeted, or stood up for, or to have his bowl or outer robe received. But a seat may be prepared for him, so that he may sit down if he likes."

But, as I approached, they weren't able to keep their prior agreement. One came to greet me and took my bowl and robe, another prepared a seat for me, and yet another set out water to wash my feet. However, they addressed me by name and as "friend."

Then I said to them, "Monks, do not address the *Tathagata* by name or as 'friend.' The *Tathagata* as fully realized—the fully enlightened one. Pay attention, friends: The deathless has been attained. I will instruct you about the *dhamma*. If you practice as you are instructed, realizing for yourselves here and now through direct knowledge, you will soon [experience] the supreme goal—that for which young men of good families rightly go forth from home life into homelessness."

When this was said the group of five monks answered me in this way: "But you, friend Gotama, through the practice…of austerities did not achieve any superhuman states, or supreme knowledge and vision worthy of a noble one. So how can you now, living decadently, having given up striving and living in luxury, have attained [these states]?"

When this was said, I replied: "The *Tathagata* does not live decadently, nor has he given up striving or reverted to a life of luxury. The *Tathagata* is fully realized—the fully enlightened one. Pay attention, friends: The deathless has been attained. I will instruct you about the *dhamma*. If you practice as you are instructed, realizing for yourselves here and now through direct knowledge, you will soon [experience] the supreme goal—that for which young men of good families rightly go forth from home life into homelessness."

And so I was able to convince them....

Then the group of five monks, having been taught by me, being themselves subject to birth, having understood the dangers involved in being subject to birth, while seeking the birthless, supreme security of *Nibbāna*, they attained the birthless, supreme security of *Nibbāna*. Being themselves subject to aging...sickness...death...sorrow...[and] defilement, having grasped the danger in what is subject to aging...sickness...death...sorrow... [and] defilement, while seeking ageless, sickless, deathless, sorrowless, undefiled, supreme security of *Nibbāna*, they attained the ageless, sickless, deathless, sorrowless, undefiled, supreme security of *Nibbāna*. This knowledge and vision arose within them: "Our liberation is complete; this is our last birth; there is no longer any becoming-again."

The Growth of the Sangha
[Vinaya Pitaka, Vol. 4: Mahavagga]

The Ordination of Rahula

Then the Blessed one after having resided at Rajagaha as long as he thought fit, went forth to Kapilavatthu....

In the morning the Blessed One, having put on his under-robes, took his alms-bowl and with his robe on went to the residence of the Sakyan Suddhodana (his father). Having gone there, he sat down in a place made ready for him.

Then the princess, who was the mother of Rahula, said to young Rahula: "This is your father, Rahula; go and ask him for your inheritance."

E. H. Brewster, ed. *The Life of Gotama the Buddha*: London: Kegan Paul, Trench, Trubner, and Co, 1926. Translation updated. Alt Trans: *The Book of the Discipline* (Vinaya-Pitaka). Vol. 4: *Mahavagga*. Trans. I.B. Horner. Oxford: Pali Text Society, 1996.

And young Rahula went to the place where the Blessed One was; having approached him, he stationed himself before the Blessed One and said: "Your shadow is a place of bliss."

Then the Blessed One rose from his seat and went away, and young Rahula followed the Blessed One from behind and said: "Give me my inheritance, Blessed One; give me my inheritance."

Then the Blessed One said to the venerable Sariputta: "Well, Sariputta confer ordination on young Rahula."

Sariputta replied: "Lord, how shall I confer ordination on young Rahula?"

In response to this question, the Blessed One, after having delivered a religious discourse, addressed the monks: "I prescribe, monks, the ordination of novices by the threefold declaration of taking refuge. You should confer ordination on a novice in this way: Let him first have his hair and beard cut off; let him put on yellow robes, adjust his upper robe so as to cover one shoulder, salute the feet of the monks with his head, and sit down squatting, then let him raise his joined hands and tell him to say: 'I take my refuge in the Buddha, I take my refuge in the dhamma, I take my refuge in the Sangha. And for the second time, etc. And for the third time...'"

"I prescribe monks, the ordination of novices by this three-fold declaration of taking refuge."

And so the venerable Sariputta conferred ordination on young Rahula.

Then the Sakyan Suddhodana went to the place where the Blessed One was. Having approached him and having respectfully saluted the Blessed One, he sat down near him and said: "Lord, I ask one favor of the Blessed One."

The Buddha replied: "The perfect ones, Gotama, are beyond granting favors."

Suddhodana said: "Lord, it is proper and blameless."

The Buddha: "Speak, Gotama."

"Lord, when the Blessed One gave up the world, it was a great pain to me; so it was when Nanda did the same; my pain was excessive when Rahula too did so....Please, lord, do not let your monks confer ordination on a son without his father's and mother's permission."

[In reply] the Blessed One said, "Monks, let no son receive ordination without his father's and mother's permission. He who confers ordination on a son without that permission, is guilty of a misdeed."

The Sangha and the Middle Path

The venerable Sona (Sona Kolivisa) soon after his higher ordination resided in the Sitavana grove.

Because of his great agitation, he was pacing up and down, his feet were wounded, and the place where he walked became covered with blood, like a slaughter-house for oxen. Then when the venerable Sona had gone apart and was deep in meditation, there arose this consideration: "Though I live as one of those disciples of the Blessed One in the practice of strenuous effort, my mind still has not been set free from its wounds through absence of craving. And at my home much wealth is stored up for me. It is both possible to enjoy that wealth and to do good deeds. Let me now, then, returning to the lower state, enjoy my wealth and do good deeds."

Now the Blessed One perceived the thought of the venerable Sona; and as quickly as a strong man can stretch forth his arm, or can draw it back again, when it has been stretched forth, he disappeared from the hill of the Vulture's Peak, and appeared in the Sitavana grove. Then the Blessed One as he was going through the sleeping-quarters, arrived with many monks where the venerable Sona had walked.

When the Blessed One saw that the place where the venerable Sona had walked was covered with blood, he said to the monks: "Whose walking place is this, monks, which is covered with blood, like a slaughterhouse for oxen?"

"Lord, while the venerable Sona was pacing up and down with great agitation, his feet were wounded; and so this place has become covered with blood...."

Then the Blessed One went to the house in which the venerable Sona was living, and there he sat down on a seat prepared for him. And the venerable Sona bowed down before the Blessed One and seated himself at one side. Then the Blessed One said to the venerable Sona: "Is it not true Sona that in your mind, when you had gone apart and were deep in meditation, there arose this thought: 'Though I have become one of those disciples of the Blessed One in the practice of strenuous effort, yet my mind has not been set free from its wounds through absence of craving. And at my house much wealth is stored up for me. It is both possible to enjoy that wealth and to do good deeds. Let me now, then, returning to the lower state enjoy my wealth and do good deeds?'"

"Yes, lord."

"What do you think then, Sona? Weren't you skilled, in playing the lute when you used to live in the world?"

"That is true, lord."

"What do you think then, Sona? When the strings of your lute were stretched too much, did it give out the proper tone and was it in a fit condition to be played upon?"

"No, lord."

"What do you think then, Sona? When the strings of your lute were too loose did it give out the proper tone and was it in a fit condition to be played upon?"

"No, lord."

"What do you think then, Sona? When the strings of your lute were neither too much stretched nor too loose, but had the proper tension, did it give out the proper tone and was it in a fit condition to be played upon?"

"Yes, lord."

"In the same way, Sona, too strenuous effort leads to overstrain, and too weak effort to sloth. Therefore, O Sona, be steadfast in evenness of effort, press through to evenness of your mental powers. Let that be the object of your thought."

"Yes, lord," said the venerable Sona, and he listened to the word of the Blessed One.

Care for Ones Fellow Monks

At one time a certain monk had an illness of the bowels, and he lay fallen in his own excrement. Now when the Blessed One, followed by the venerable Ananda, was passing by the sleeping quarters he came to the cell of that monk and saw him in such a condition. And seeing he went to him and said: "What is it, monk, are you ill?"

"I have an illness of the bowels, lord."

"Have you no one to care for you, monk?"

"No, lord."

"Why don't the monks care for you?"

"Because, lord, I am of no service to the monks."

After hearing this, the Blessed One said to the venerable Ananda: "Ananda, go and bring some water, let us bathe this monk."

"Yes, lord," replied the venerable Ananda to the Blessed One, and brought the water. Then the Blessed One poured the water, while the venerable Ananda washed him. And the Blessed One holding him by the head, and the venerable Ananda by the feet, they lifted him and laid him down upon his bed.

Then on that occasion and in that connection, the Blessed One called a gathering of the Order, and asked the monks: "Monks, in such and such a quarter is there a monk who is sick?"

"Yes, lord."

"And, monks, what is the matter with that monk?"

"He has an illness of the bowels, lord."

"And is there no one to care for him, monks?"

"No, lord."

"But why do not the monks care for him?"

"Lord, that monk is of no service to his fellow monks, and therefore they do not care for him."

"Monks, you have no mothers or fathers who might care for you. If you do not care for one another, who indeed will care for you? Monks, whoever would care for me should care for the sick. If he has a preceptor his preceptor should care for him as long as his life lasts until he is recovered, and the same if he has a teacher, a co-disciple of the same monastery or a disciple lodging with his teacher. And if he has none of these, then the Sangha should care for him; and whoever does not do so, shall be guilty of offence."

Admission of Women into the Sangha

Now at that time the Blessed Buddha was staying among the Sakyas in Kapilavatthu, in the Nigrodharama. And Mahapajapati Gotami (the Buddha's stepmother) went to the place where the Blessed One was, and on arriving there, bowed down before the Blessed One, and remained standing on one side. And so standing she spoke to the Blessed One:

"It would be a good thing, lord, if women should be allowed to renounce their homes and enter the homeless state under the doctrine and discipline proclaimed by the Tathagata."

"Enough, Gotami. You should not ask that women be allowed to do so."

(And a second and a third time Mahapajapati made the same request in the same words, and received the same reply.)....

Then Mahapajapati, sad and sorrowful that the Blessed One would not permit women to enter the homeless state, bowed down before the Blessed One, and keeping him on her right hand as she passed him, departed in tears.

Now when the Blessed One had remained at Kapilavatthu as long as he desired, he set out on his journey towards Vesali; and traveling straight on in due course arrived there. And there at Vesali the Blessed One stayed, in the Mahavana in the Kutagara Hall.

And Mahapajapati cut off her hair, and put on orange-coloured robes, and set out, with a number of women of the Sakya clan, towards Vesali; and in due course she arrived at Vesali, at the Mahavana, at the Kutagara Hall. And Mahapajapati, with swollen feet and covered with dust, sad and sorrowful, in tears took her stand outside under the entrance porch.

And the venerable Ananda saw her so standing there, and on

seeing her so he said to Mahapajapati: "Why do you stand there, outside the porch, with swollen feet and covered with dust, sad and sorrowful, in tears?

"Because, Ananda, as the lord, the Blessed One, does not permit women to renounce their homes and enter the homeless state under the doctrine and discipline proclaimed by the Tathagata."

Upon hearing this, the venerable Ananda went to the place where the Blessed One was, bowed down before him, and took his seat on one side. Then the venerable Ananda said to the Blessed One: "Look, lord, Mahapajapati is standing outside under the entrance porch, with swollen feet and covered with dust, sad and sorrowful, in tears because the Blessed One does not permit women to renounce their homes and enter the homeless state under the doctrine and discipline proclaimed by the Blessed One. It would be a good thing, lord, if women were to have permission granted to them to do as she desires."

"Enough, Ananda. You should not ask that women be allowed to do so."

(And a second and a third time Ananda made the same request, in the same words, and received the same reply.)...

Then the venerable Ananda thought: The Blessed One does not give his permission. Let me now ask the Blessed One on another ground

And the venerable Ananda said to the Blessed One: "Are women, lord, capable when they have gone forth from the household life and entered the homeless state, under the doctrine and discipline proclaimed by the Blessed One are they capable of realizing the fruit of conversion, or of the second Path, or of the third Path, or of Enlightenment itself?"

"They are capable, Ananda."

"Lord, if they are capable of all this, since Mahapajapati has proved herself of great service to the Blessed One, when as aunt and nurse she nourished him and gave him milk, and on the death of his mother suckled the Blessed One at her own breast, it would be a good thing, lord, that women should have permission to go forth from the household life and enter the homeless state under the doctrine and discipline proclaimed by the *Tathagata.*"

"If then, Ananda, Mahapajapati takes upon herself the eight chief rules of the order, let that be regarded by her as her ordination."

CHAPTER III

Last Days of the Buddha

The Buddha was said to have spent 45 years wandering through northern India, preaching the dhamma, administering his ever-growing communities of monks and nuns, and helping to settle political disputes between warring factions. As he approached his 80th year, however, the Buddha began to feel the effects of old age, describing himself as an old cart that can barely manage to hold itself together without the help of leather straps (DN 16.2.25, p. 245). At this point the question was put to him by Ananda, his cousin and attendant, as to who would lead the order after the Buddha was gone. The Buddha's answer was that there was no need for a successor, since the teachings that he shared during the course of his life should continue to guide his followers. "Therefore," he instructed his monks, "...you should live as islands unto yourselves, being your own refuge, with no one else as your refuge, with the *dhamma* as an island, with the *dhamma* as your refuge, with no other refuge" (DN 16.2.26, p. 245).

One day, while he was travelling through the town of Pava, he stopped at the mango grove of a blacksmith named Cunda. He accepted food offered to him by Cunda and was struck with a severe illness from what may have been tainted pork. Whether he died as a result of this meal or from natural causes later on, from that moment on the Buddha's days were numbered.

As he prepared for his death (*parinibbana;* literally "final extinction"), the Buddha was moved to the town of Kusinagari to be with monks. Lying between two Sal trees, the Buddha asked his monks if they had any doubts about his teachings. "Ask monks!" he admonished. "Do no later on have remorse thinking, 'The teacher was right there before us and we did not ask [him] face to face'" (DN 16.6.5, p. 270). Content that his teachings were understood by his disciples, the Buddha then uttered his last words: "Now monks, I declare to you: all conditioned things are of a nature to decay—strive on untiringly." (DN: 16.6.7, p. 270). Shortly after making this exhortation, the Buddha slipped into a coma, and during the night he died.

After the Buddha

After the Buddha's death, his followers convened a series of councils to settle disputes as to what exactly the Buddha had taught. The first of these took place a year after the Buddha's death in the city of Rajagriha. It was at this council that the Buddha's teachings were preserved and his monastic code further developed.

In 80 BCE one of the most important Buddhist councils took place at Anuradhapura on the island of Sri Lanka, where Buddhist monks gathered approximately 400 years after the death of their founder to decide upon an authentic body of Buddhist scripture. Prior to this point, the teachings of the Buddha had been preserved by means of oral tradition, primarily through communal chanting in monasteries. After months of debate, an essential body of the Buddha's teaching was decided upon and committed to writing. This collection that resulted has come to be known as the Pali Canon, because Pali is the language of these early texts. The Pali Canon consists of three divisions or "baskets" (*pitaka*) which includes the *Vinaya,* a collection of texts containing rules for monks and nuns, the *Nikayas*, collections of suttas, or teachings, attributed to the Buddha, and the *Abhidhamma*, a collection of texts which develop the philosophical and psychological underpinnings of the teachings of the Buddha.

Buddhism continued to flourish in India in the centuries following the Buddha's death, with Buddhist monasteries spreading throughout the subcontinent. The religion reached its pinnacle of growth during the reign of the Emperor Asoka, whose empire extended throughout most of India during the 3rd century BCE. In an attempt to consolidate his power, in 260 Ashoka waged a fierce war against the state of Kalinga that was so shockingly destructive that he gradually began to convert to Buddhism as a result. Recognizing that Buddhism could be a unifying factor throughout his empire, Ashoka committed himself to the spread of Buddhism throughout India, funding monasteries, building numerous stupas (shrines to the Buddha) and erecting hundreds of rock pillars throughout his empire in which Buddhist principles were inscribed. Perhaps the Emperor's most important legacy was his sponsorship of Buddhist missionary activity that enabled Buddhism to gain a foothold in places like Sri Lanka and Burma, ensuring that the religion would survive even after Buddhist institutions had all but disappeared in India by the 13th century CE as a result of Muslim invasion beginning in the 11th century and Hindu persecutions of Buddhism.

Even as Buddhism was dying out in India, however, it began to take root throughout Asia. The spread of the *dhamma* followed the Buddha's admonition to his disciples to "go and travel around for the welfare of the multitudes, for the happiness of the multitudes, out of sympathy for the world, for the benefit, welfare, and happiness of gods and humans. No two should go in the same direction" (V 1.20-21, p. 28). Essentially two main branches of Buddhism established themselves in Asia. Southern or Theravada Buddhism took hold in Sri Lanka, Thailand, Cambodia, Burma, and Laos; Northern or Mahayana Buddhism established itself in China, Japan, Korea, Vietnam and Tibet.

READING THE SOURCES

The Buddha's Last Days
[Mahaparinibbana Sutta]

The Dhamma as Sole Refuge

When the Blessed One had stayed so long as he wished at Ambapali's grove...[he went] with a great company of the monks to Beluva, where he stayed. There the Blessed One said to the monks: "You monks should go to Vesali, where you have friends and companions, and spend the rainy season there. For my part, I will spend the rainy season here at Beluva...."

During the rainy season, the Blessed One experienced a severe sickness, with sharp pains as if he were about to die. But the Blessed One, mindful and self-possessed, bore them without complaint. Then this thought occurred to him: "It would not be right for me to pass away without addressing the disciples and without taking leave of the Order. Let me now, by a strong effort of the will keep this sickness in check and hold on to life." And his sickness abated.

After he had recovered and began to feel better, he came out from his lodging and sat on a seat in the open air. Then the venerable Ananda came to him, greeted him, sat down to one side and said: "I have seen the Blessed One in health and I have seen how the Blessed One had to suffer. At the sight of the sickness of the Blessed One, my body became weakened, and I lost my bearing,

---

E. H. Brewster, ed. *The Life of Gotama the Buddha*: London: Kegan Paul, Trench, Trubner, and Co, 1926. Translation updated. Alt Trans: DN 16, pp. 231-277.

and things were unclear to me. And yet I took some comfort from the thought that the Blessed One would not pass away until at least he had left instructions concerning the Order."

"What then, Ananda, does the Order expect of me? I have preached the dhamma without making distinctions between teachings hidden and revealed. The *Tathagata* has no such thing as the teacher's closed fist with respect to doctrines. If there is anyone who thinks, 'I should lead the order' or 'The Order is dependent upon me,' it is he who should lay down instructions in any matter concerning the Order. But the Tathagata does not think in such terms. Why then should he leave instructions concerning the order?"

"Ananda, I have grown old, and full of years, my journey is drawing to its close, I have reached the summit of my days, being over eighty years old. Just as a worn-out cart, Ananda, can be kept going only with the help of straps, so the body of the Tathagata can only be kept going by being strapped up. It is only when the Tathagata, ceases to pay attention to outward things... and enters into the concentration of mind that his body is at ease."

"Therefore, Ananda, be islands unto yourselves. Be a refuge to yourselves and rely on no other refuge. Hold fast to the *dhamma* as an island. Hold fast as a refuge to the *dhamma*. Look not for refuge to any one besides yourselves. And how, Ananda, is a brother to be an island a unto himself, a refuge to himself with no other refuge, holding fast to the *dhamma* as an island, holding fast as a refuge to the *dhamma*, looking not for refuge to any one besides himself?"

"Herein, Ananda, a monk abides, contemplating the body as body, clearly aware, mindful, having overcome both desire and aversion for the world. And in the same way with regard to sensations, mind-states, and mind-objects...."

"And whosoever, Ananda, either now or after I am dead, shall be islands unto themselves, and a refuge unto themselves with no other refuge, but holding fast to the *dhamma* as their island, and holding fast as their refuge to the *dhamma*, shall look not for a refuge to any one besides themselves, it is they, Ananda, among my monks, who shall become the highest, if they are willing to learn."

The Buddha Accepts Food from Chunda

The Blessed One proceeded with a large company of monks to Pava, where he stayed at the mango grove of Chunda, the smith...Hearing of his arrival, Chunda went to the place where the Blessed One was, and greeting him took his seat respectfully on one side. And when he was seated, the Exalted One instructed, aroused, incited and gladdened him with a discourse on the dhamma.

Then Cunda said: "May the Blessed One do me the honor of taking a meal together with his monks at my house tomorrow?"

...Seeing that the Exalted One had consented, Chunda rose from his seat, bowed down before the Blessed One, and...departed.

As the night was ending, Chunda made a fine meal of sweet rice and cakes with an abundance of tender pork. And when it was ready, he announced, "Lord, the hour has come and the meal is ready."

Then the Blessed One, having clothed himself early in the morning, took his bowl in hand and went to the home of Chunda, where he seated himself in preparation for the meal and said: "Serve the pork that has been prepared to me, and serve the remaining sweet rice and cakes to the others."

"Certainly, Lord," said Chunda, and did as he was told.

Then the Blessed One said to Chunda: "Whatever pork is left over bury in a hole, because I can see none in this world...who, if they were to eat it, could properly digest it, except a *Tathagata*."

"Certainly, Lord," said Chunda. And whatever pork remained, he buried in a hole. Then he went to the place where the Blessed One was and took his seat respectfully on one side. And when he was seated, the Blessed One instructed and aroused and incited and gladdened Chunda with a discourse on the *dhamma*. When he was finished, the Blessed One then rose from his seat and departed.

After having eaten the meal prepared by Chunda, the Blessed One was attacked by a severe sickness, the disease of dysentery, with sharp pains as if he were about to die. But the Blessed One, mindful and self-possessed, bore it without complaint. And the

Blessed One addressed the venerable Ananda, and said: "Come, Ananda, let us go on to Kusinara."

"Very well, Lord," said Ananda to the Exalted One.

The Last Words of the Buddha

And the Blessed One said to Ananda: "It may be, Ananda, that some of you will think: 'The teacher's instruction has ended; no longer do we have a teacher.' But it should not be seen like this. Let the *dhamma*, and the Rules of the Order, which I have set forth and laid down for you all, be your teacher.

"When I am gone, do not address one another as you have in the past as "friend." A younger brother may be addressed by an elder by name, or his family name, or as 'friend.' But an elder should be addressed by a younger brother as 'Sir' or as 'Venerable Sir.'

"When I am gone, Ananda, if it should wish, let the order abolish the minor rules...."

Then the Exalted One addressed the monks, saying: "It may be, monks, that there may be doubt or misgiving in the mind of some brother as to the Buddha, or the *dhamma*, or the *sangha*, or the path, or the method. Inquire, monks, freely. Do not have to reproach yourselves afterwards with the thought: 'Our teacher was face to face with us, and we could not bring ourselves to inquire of the Blessed One when we were before him.'"

At these words, the monks were silent.

And again the second and the third time the Exalted One addressed the monks, and said: "It may be, monks, that there may be doubt or misgiving in the mind of some brother as to the Buddha, or the *dhamma*, or the *sangha*, or the path, or the method. Inquire, monks, freely. Do not have to reproach yourselves afterwards with the thought: 'Our teacher was face to face with us, and we could not bring ourselves to inquire of the Blessed One when we were before him.'"

And even the third time the monks were silent.

Then the Blessed One addressed the brethren, and said: "It may be, monks, that you do not ask out of respect for the teacher. Then monks, let one friend communicate to another."

And still the monks were silent.

And the venerable Ananda said to the Blessed One: "How wonderful a thing is it, Lord, and how marvelous. I truly believe that in this whole assembly there is not one monk who has any doubt or misgiving as to the Buddha, or the dhamma, or the sangha, or the path, or the method."

"It is out of the fullness of faith that you speak, Ananda. But the *Tathagata* knows for certain that in this whole assembly of the brethren there is not one brother who has any doubt or misgiving as to the Buddha, or the *dhamma*, or the *sangha*, or the path, or the method. For even the least of all these five hundred brethren has become converted, is no longer liable to be born in a state of suffering, and is assured of hereafter attaining to the Enlightenment."

Then the Exalted One addressed the brethren, and said: "Now, monks, I declare to you: 'All conditioned things are subject to decay. Strive unceasingly!'"

These were the last words of the Tathagata.

The Death of the Buddha

Then the Blessed One entered into the first stage of Rapture (*jhāna*). And rising out of the first stage he passed into the second. And rising out of the second, he passed into the third. And rising out of the third stage he passed into the fourth. And rising out of the fourth stage of Rapture, he entered into the state of mind to which the infinity of space is alone present. And passing out of the mere consciousness of the infinity of space he entered into the state of mind to which the infinity of thought is alone present. And passing out of the mere consciousness of the infinity of thought, he entered into a state of mind to which nothing at all was specially present. And passing out of the consciousness of no special object he fell into a state between consciousness and unconsciousness. And passing out of the state between consciousness and unconsciousness he fell into a state in which the consciousness both of sensations and of ideas had wholly passed away.

Then the venerable Ananda said to the venerable Anuruddha: "Lord, Anuruddha, the Blessed One is dead."

"No, friend Ananda, the Exalted One is not dead. He has entered into that state in which both sensations and ideas have ceased to be."

Then the Blessed One, passing out of the state in which both sensations and ideas have ceased to be, entered into the state between consciousness and unconsciousness. And passing out of the state between consciousness and unconsciousness he entered into the state of mind to which nothing at all is specially present. And passing out of the consciousness of no special object he entered into the state of mind to which the infinity of thought is alone present. And passing out of the mere consciousness of the infinity of thought he entered into the state of mind to which the infinity of space is alone present. And passing out of the mere consciousness of the infinity of space he entered into the fourth stage of Rapture. And passing out of the fourth he entered into the third. And passing out of the third stage he entered into the second. And passing out of the second he entered into the first. And passing out of the first stage of Rapture he entered into the second. And passing out of the second stage he entered into the third. And passing out of the third stage he entered into the fourth stage of Rapture. And passing out of the last stage of Rapture he finally passed away.

Emaciated Buddha (Gandhara, Pakistan, 2nd - 3rd centuries)

CHAPTER IV

The Buddha's Methodology

Having examined the life of the Buddha in some detail, we can now begin to examine his teachings. Just as there are difficulties in ascertaining which of the stories we have about the Buddha's life are historically accurate or not, we have a similar difficulty when attempting to construct an authentic philosophy of Buddhism. With the rise of Mahayana Buddhism and those traditions most closely associated with it—most notably Zen and Tibetan Buddhism—Buddhist thought evolved to fit into the new cultures (China, Japan, and Tibet in which it found itself. To determine what the Buddha himself actually taught (as opposed to later embellishments on his thought), we'll try to adhere fairly closely to the evidence presented in the Pali Canon and other early Buddhist sources in this chapter and in the following two.

Before we get to what most people probably consider the core of the Buddha's teaching—the Four Noble Truths and the Eightfold Path—it's vital to understand the basic philosophical approach adopted by the Buddha. In this chapter, therefore, we'll explore the methodology employed by the Buddha to determine which sorts of questions are worth exploring and which are not, and in the next the basic understanding of reality that underlies his thought.

One of the reasons why some scholars hesitate to refer to Buddhism as a religion and prefer to call it a philosophy of life is that Buddhism doesn't really seem to fit the characteristics of most of the world's major religions. The Buddha never taught the existence of a personal god or gods. The practice he shared with his followers involved no prayer, no worship, no ritual, and little or no ceremony. The Buddha himself never claimed to be a god or savior or to have any special powers to intercede in the affairs of human beings, either before or after his death. There's no concept of sin as commonly understood and no external system of rewards and punishments in his thought. Finally, there doesn't even seem to be any concept of an afterlife in the earliest traditions of Buddhism, since the Buddha flatly rejected the possibility of any kind of enduring self. If Buddhism is a religion, then it is a very strange sort of religion indeed!

Noble Silence

In fact, throughout the suttas, the Buddha consistently avoids engaging in the kind of metaphysical talk that is commonly found in the sacred texts of all of the world's major religions. For example, in one story, the wanderer Vacchagotta asks Buddha a series of metaphysical questions, including whether the world is eternal or not, whether it is finite or infinite, whether the soul and body are the same, and whether one who has attained nirvana continues to exist after death. In response, the Buddha simply refuses to answer any of these questions. Why the reticence on his part? The answer that he does give to Vacchagotta is illuminating. Holding metaphysical views, he says, is a "thicket of views, a wilderness of views, a contortion of views, a vacillation of views, a filter of views. It is beset by suffering, by vexation…and it does not lead to…peace, to direct knowledge, to enlightenment, to *Nibbāna*….Seeing this danger, I do not take up any of these [metaphysical] views" (MN 72.14, p. 591). This text is certainly not unique: throughout the Pali Cannon, the Buddha consistently and unequivocally maintained his "noble silence" on such matters.

The reason for the Buddha's silence on these issues has three possible explanations: (1) It may very well be the case that the Buddha was an agnostic on these sorts of issues, and therefore didn't have a positive position to offer his followers. (2) He may have been a proto-atheist and was so far out of the mainstream of his time in rejecting common religious ideas like karma and reincarnation that he knew his true views would never be accepted. (3) Whatever views he may have held himself, he thought that these sorts of issues were fundamentally irrelevant and therefore not worth discussing.

Although there are those scholars like Steve Hagen (*Buddhism is Not What You Think*), who argues persuasively for the agnostic position, and Stephen Batchelor (*Confessions of a Buddhist Atheist*), who in recent years has developed a provocative atheistic interpretation of the Buddha's thought, their arguments seem to go beyond the evidence presented in the Pali Canon. We cannot know what the Buddha actually thought about what he called "speculative views" precisely because of his rigid adherence to noble silence on these subjects. Hagan and Batchelor are to be credited, however, for helping us to realize that there is no inherent contradiction between being an agnostic, or even an atheist, and being a Buddhist.

There is ample evidence, however, for the third position. This sort of interpretation argues that it basically doesn't matter what the Buddha himself believed about metaphysical and religious issues, because he himself didn't see these issues as all that important to his central mission—the alleviation of suffering. For example, in the text, "Questions that Do Not Tend to Edify," (*Shorter Malunkyaputta Sutta*) the wandering monk Malunkyaputta approaches the Buddha and asks a series of ten metaphysical questions similar to those posed by Vacchagotta. He even threatens to stop following the Buddha if he doesn't answer his questions. The Buddha responded to this monk's questions by using a metaphor of a man shot with an arrow, arguing that, if one were shot with an arrow and critically wounded, a sensible individual wouldn't go around asking a lot of irrelevant questions concerning the person who shot the arrow or the specific design of the arrow itself. "All this would still not be known to that [wounded] man and meanwhile he would die" (MN 63.5, p. 534). Similarly, metaphysical questions like those asked by Malunkyaputta, the Buddha argued, are best left unexamined because they are "unedifying"— in other words, they do not help to relieve a person's suffering. When pressed on metaphysical questions, the Buddha would say that all he taught was "suffering and the cessation of suffering" (MN 22.38, p. 234).

For many spiritual types, questions like whether a God or gods exist, whether his soul lives on after death, or whether there is some kind of punishment after death for personal sins seem to be fundamental existential and religious problems. Indeed, if one reads the major texts of the world's great religions—Hinduism, Judaism, Christianity, and Islam—questions like these seem to arise all the time. This is most assuredly not the case in Buddhism—or at least not the Buddhism taught by Buddha himself. Whatever his own views were regarding such questions, in the end the Buddha clearly didn't think that they were significant enough to spend time obsessing over. For one thing, we can have no true certainty with regards to the answers to such questions: at best all we can have is idle speculation. But even more importantly, he regarded such questions as essentially "unedifying". Even if we could find out the answers to these questions, they wouldn't help us to resolve the ultimate question in life: how can we alleviate the suffering in our lives. And the answer to this question, as we shall see, doesn't involve any idle speculation at all.

Buddhist Skepticism

It's significant to note even with respect to those issues that he considered of great importance—problems related to suffering and its eradication—the Buddha encouraged an attitude of radical skepticism from all of his followers. Nothing was to be accepted dogmatically.

In the *Kalama Sutta*, for example, the Kalamas go to the Buddha complaining about the fact that they've been visited by many religious teachers, each of whom promotes his own teachings and attacks the teachings of others. In the end, they claim to be "perplexed and in doubt" about what they have heard. Rather than attempting to dispel their doubt, the Buddha surprisingly congratulates them on it, saying, "It is fitting for you to be perplexed, Kalamas, fitting for you to be in doubt." "Doubt," he says, "has arisen in you [precisely about what ought to be doubted]." He then goes on to encourage them to reject all tradition, all custom, all sacred texts, and all authority when attempting to discern between what is true and what is false (AN 1.65, p. 280).

But what about the Buddha's own teachings? Shouldn't these at least be accepted absolutely, as matters of faith? The answer amazingly is no. The Buddha tells his followers that his own teachings are "similar to a raft, for the purpose of crossing over, not for the purpose of grasping" (MN 22.13, p. 228). The *dhamma*, he maintains, is a means, not an end in itself; it should be used as a guide and a resource that can assist us in our quest for enlightenment, but should never be clung to dogmatically. When we no longer find these teachings useful or helpful in alleviating our human suffering, they can be discarded. Implicit in the Buddha's teachings is the idea that one should be skeptical with respect to the ideas of *all* teachers and authority figures—and this most certainly includes himself.

So if we are called to question all teaching, all authority, and all scripture, what then can we possibly use as a guide to help us determine what is true or false? In the *Kalama Sutta*, the Buddha urges us to use experience as our guide. "[W]hen you know for yoursel[f]," he says, that certain things lead to the happiness of oneself and others, then you should do these things; and "when you know for yoursel[f]" that certain things lead to the suffering of oneself and others, you should avoid doing them (AN 1.65, p. 280-282). Instead of relying on any outside sources of authority at all, the Buddha calls on us to rely on our own direct experience and trust our own innate wisdom to guide us. In place of speculative views, he calls us to begin looking at the world with "direct vision" or seeing things as they really are (MN 72.15, p. 592). This direct vision into the true nature of existence, as we shall see, is the key to the Buddha's entire philosophical system.

READING THE SOURCES

Unedifying Questions
[Shorter Malunkyaputta Sutta]

Thus have I heard.

On a certain occasion the Blessed One was dwelling at Savatthi in Jetavana monastery in Anathapindika's Park. While the venerable Malunkyaputta was secluded in meditation, the following thought arose in his mind: "These theories which The Blessed One has left unclarified and has set aside and rejected: that the world is eternal, that the world is not eternal, that the world is finite, that the world is infinite, that the soul and the body are identical, that the soul is one thing and the body another, that a Tathagata exists after death, that a Tathagata does not exist after death, that a Tathagata both exists and does not exist after death, that a Tathagata neither exists nor does not exist after death."

The Blessed One has not clarified these to me and this does not please me nor suit me. Therefore I will go to the Blessed One and inquire concerning this matter. If The Blessed One will clarify me [on these matters] then I will lead the religious life under The Blessed One. If The Blessed One will not clarify me [on these matters] then I abandon religious training and return to the lower life of a layman."

When it was evening the venerable Malunkyaputta arose at eventide from his seclusion, and went to the Blessed One. After paying his respects, he sat down to one side and said to the Blessed One: "Venerable One, while I was secluded in meditation, the following thought arose in my mind: These theories have been

---

Henry Clarke Warren, trans. "The Lesser Malunkyaputta Sutta." *Buddhism in Translation*. Cambridge: Harvard University Press, 1896. Translation updated. Alt Trans: MN 63, pp. 533-536.

left unclarified by the Blessed One….It does not please or suit me that the Blessed One has not seen fit to clarify these matters for me…. If The Blessed One will not clarify me [on these matters] then I abandon religious training and return to the lower life of a layman. If the Blessed One knows the world is eternal, or the world is not eternal, let the Blessed One clarify this for me; if the Blessed one does not know whether either that the world is eternal or the world is not eternal, the only right response for one who does not know, or who does not have that insight, is to say, 'I do not know; I do not have that insight."

"If The Blessed One knows that the world is finite…."

"If The Blessed One knows that the soul and body are identical…."

"If The Blessed One knows that a Tathagata exists after death…."

"If The Blessed One knows that a Tathagata both exists and does not exist after death, let The Blessed One clarify me [on these matters]…."

"Malunkyaputta, did I ever say to you, 'Come, Malunkyaputta, lead the religious life under me, and I will clarify for you either that the world is eternal, or that the world is not eternal,…or that a Tatagatha neither exists nor does not exist after death'?"

"No, Venerable One."

"Or did you ever say to me, 'Venerable One, I will lead the religious life under The Blessed One on condition that The Blessed One clarify for me whether the world is eternal or that the world is not eternal,….or that a Tathagata neither exists nor does not exist after death'?"

"No, Venerable One."

"So you acknowledge, [this] Malunkyaputta….That being the case, foolish man, why are you so angry and claiming grievances of anyone?

"Malunkyaputta, anyone who should say, 'I will not lead a religious life under the Blessed One until the Blessed One shall clarify for me either that the world is eternal, or that the world is not eternal,…or that a Tathagata neither exists nor does not exist after death;'—that person would die, Malunkyaputta, before The Tathagata had ever clarified this for him.

"It is as if, Malunkyaputta, a man had been wounded by an arrow thickly smeared with poison, and his friends and companions, his relatives and kinsfolk, brought a surgeon to treat him; and that man would say, 'I will not have this arrow taken out until I have learnt whether the man who wounded me belonged to the warrior caste, or to the Brahman caste, or to the agricultural caste, or to the menial caste...or until I have learnt the name of the man who wounded me, and to what clan he belongs...or until I have learnt whether the man who wounded me was tall, or short, or of the middle height...or until I have learnt whether the man who wounded me was black, brown, or of yellow skinned...or until I have learnt whether the man who wounded me was from this or that village, or town, or city...or until I have learnt whether the bow which wounded me was a longbow or a crossbow...or until I have learnt [what material] the bow-strings [were made from].... or until I have learnt whether the shaft which wounded me was a wild or a cultivated...or until I have learnt whether the shaft which wounded me was feathered from the wings of a vulture, a heron, a falcon, a peacock, or of a stork...or until I have learnt how the shaft which wounded me was bound...or until I have learnt how the arrow which wounded me was [fashioned]."

"All this would remain unknown to the man and meanwhile he would die. In the same way, Malunkyaputta, anyone who should say, 'I will not lead the religious life under The Blessed One until The Blessed One shall clarify for me either that the world is eternal, or that the world is not eternal,...or that a Tathagata neither exists nor does not exist after death;'—that person would die, Malunkyaputta, before the Tathagata had ever clarified this for him.

"The religious life, Malunkyaputta, does not depend on the dogma that the world is eternal; nor does the religious life depend on the dogma that the world is not eternal. Whether one holds that the world is eternal or that the world is not eternal, there is still birth, old age, death, sorrow, lamentation, misery, grief, and despair, for the extinction of which I am prescribing here and now....

"Therefore, Malunkyaputta, always remember what I have left unclarified and what I have clarified. And what, Malunkyaputta, have I not clarified? I have not clarified, Malunkyaputta, that the world is eternal; I have not clarified that the world is not eternal; I have not clarified that the world is finite; I have not clarified that the world is infinite; I have not clarified that the soul and the body are identical; I have not clarified that the soul is one thing and the body another; I have not clarifed that the saint exists after death; I have not clarified that a Tathagata does not exist after death; I have not clarified that a Tathagata both exists and does not exist after death; I have not clarified that a Tathagata neither exists nor does not exist after death.

"And why have I not clarified these things? Because they do not benefit anyone and they do not belong to the fundamentals of the religious life; nor do they lead to disengagement, dispassion, to cessation, to peace, to calming, to awakening, to enlightenment, to Nibbana. Therefore I have not clarified these things.

"And what have I clarified? I've clarified, 'This is suffering.' I've clarified, 'This is the origin of suffering.' I've clarified, 'This is the cessation of suffering.' I've clarified, 'This is the path leading to the cessation of suffering.'

"Why have I clarified these things? Because they are of benefit and they belong to the fundamentals of the religious life; also because they lead to disengagement, to dispassion, to cessation, to peace, to calming, to awakening, to enlightenment, to Nibbana. Therefore I have clarified these things.

"Therefore, Malunkyaputta, always remember what I have left unclarified and what I have clarified."

This is what the Blessed One said. And the Venerable Malunkyaputta was gratified and delighted by his words.

The Analogy of the Raft
[Alagaddupama Sutta]

"Monks, I will show you how the dhamma is similar to a raft: it is for the purpose of crossing over, not for clinging to. Listen, monks, to what I have to tell you."

"Yes, Venerable One," the monks said.

"Suppose a man were on a journey and he sees a great expanse of water. The nearby shore is perilous and risky, while the opposite shore is secure and free from danger. But there is no ferryboat or bridge going from one side to the other. It occurs to

---

Alt Trans: MN 22.13, pp. 228-229.

him, '[Given this situation], what if I gather grass, sticks, branch-es, and leaves and bind them together to form a raft, and direct it with my hands and feet in order to cross over into safety.' Then the man gathered grass, sticks, branches, and leaves and binds them together to form a raft. Carried by that raft, which he directs by his hands and feet, he safely crosses over to the other shore. Having crossed over to the other shore, it occurs to him, 'This raft has indeed been very useful to me, since…it allowed me to cross over and get to the other shore. Shouldn't I hoist it onto my head or shoulders and take it with me wherever I go?'

"What do you think, monks: Would the man be correct in do-ing what he did with the raft?"

"No, Venerable One."

"Well, then, monks, what should the man be doing with that raft? When the man got to the other shore, it might [instead] oc-cur to him: "This raft has indeed been very useful to me since… it allowed me to cross over and get to the other shore. Shouldn't I just hoist it onto dry land or allow it to drift away, and then go wherever I like?" By acting in this way, monks, that man would be doing what he should with the raft.

In the same way, monks, I have shown you how the *dhamma* is similar to a raft—for the purpose of crossing over, not for clinging to."

Instructions to the Kalamas
[Kalama Sutta]

Thus have I heard.

On one occasion the Blessed One was on a walk among the Kosalanas with a large group of monks and entered a town of the Kalamas called Kesaputta. The Kalamas of Kesaputta had heard, "This Gotama, the ascetic of the Sakyan clan, has gone forth and has arrived in Kesaputta. A good report about Master Gotama has spread, saying, 'This Blessed One is a worthy one, perfectly enlightened…and he reveals a spiritual life that is com-

---

Alt Trans: AN 65.5, pp. 279-283.

pletely pure.' Seeing such worthy ones is good indeed."
Then the Kalamas of Kesaputta approached the Blessed One.
[After paying homage to him and sitting down], the Kalamas said
to the Blessed One: "Venerable One, there are some ascetics and
brahmins who come to Kesaputta. They explain and expound
their own doctrines while at the same time disparaging, reviling,
and denigrating, and denouncing the doctrines of others. We are
perplexed and in doubt concerning which of these good ascetics
and brahmins speak the truth and which speak falsehood."

The Experiential Criterion

"Kalamas it is fitting for you to be in doubt and uncertain. Doubt
has arisen in you about what is uncertain. Come, Kalamas. Do not
go based upon oral tradition, nor upon tradition, nor upon rumor,
nor upon what is written in scriptures, nor upon logical reasoning,
nor upon axiom, nor upon biased deductions, nor upon the perceived competence of a speaker, nor upon the idea, 'This monk
is our teacher.' Kalamas, when you know yourself, 'These things
are bad, these things are blameworthy, these things are repudiated
by the wise; when accepted and undertaken, these things lead to
harm and suffering,' then you should abandon them."

Greed, Hatred, and Delusion

"What do you think, Kalamas? Does greed arise in a person for
his benefit or his harm?"
"For his harm, Venerable One."
"Kalamas, being given over to greed, obsessed by greed, overcome mentally by greed, a person destroys life, steals, commits
adultery, and tells lies, and encourages others to do likewise. Will
that lead to his long-term harm and suffering?"
"Yes, Venerable One."
"What do you think, Kalamas? Does hatred arise in a person
for his benefit or his harm?"
"For his harm, Venerable One."
"Kalamas, being given over to hatred, obsessed by greed,
overcome mentally by greed, a person destroys life, steals, com-

mits adultery, and tells lies, and encourages others to do likewise. Will that lead to his long-term harm and suffering?"

"Yes, Venerable One."

"What do you think, Kalamas? Does delusion arise in a person for his benefit or his harm?"

"For his harm, Venerable One."

"Kalamas, being given over to delusion, obsessed by greed, overcome mentally by greed, a person destroys life, steals, commits adultery, and tells lies, and encourages others to do likewise. Will that lead to his long-term harm and suffering?"

"Yes, Venerable One."

"What do you think, Kalama? Are these things good or bad?"

"Bad, Venerable One."

"Blameworthy or blameless?"

"Blameworthy, Venerable One."

"Censured or praised by the wise?"

"Censured by the wise, Venerable One."

"Accepted and undertaken, do they lead to harm and suffering or not?"

"Accepted and undertaken, they lead to harm and suffering. So it strikes us."

"Therefore Kalamas, do not go based upon oral tradition, etc....But when you know yourself, 'These things are bad, these things are blameworthy, these things are repudiated by the wise; when accepted and undertaken, these things lead to harm and suffering,' then you should abandon them."

The Absence of Greed, Hatred, and Delusion

"Come, Kalamas. Do not go based upon oral tradition, etc..... Kalamas, when you know yourself, 'These things are good, these things are blameless, these things are praised by the wise; when accepted and undertaken, these things lead to well-being and happiness,' then you should live in accordance with them."

"What do you think, Kalamas. Does the absence of greed arise in a person for his benefit or his harm?"

"For his benefit, Venerable One."

"Kalamas, being not given over to greed, not obsessed by

greed, not overcome mentally by greed, a person does not destroy life, does not steal, does not commit adultery, and does not tell lies, and does not encourage others to do likewise. Will that lead to his long-term well-being and happiness?"

"Yes, Venerable One."

"What do you think, Kalamas? Does the absence of hatred arise in a person for his benefit or his harm?"

"For his benefit, Venerable One."

"Kalamas, being not given over to hatred, not obsessed by hatred, not overcome mentally by hatred, a person does not destroy life, does not steal, does not commit adultery, and does not tell lies, and does not encourage others to do likewise. Will that lead to his long-term well-being and happiness?"

"Yes, Venerable One."

"What do you think, Kalamas? Does the absence of delusion arise in a person for his benefit or his harm?"

"For his benefit, Venerable One."

"Kalamas, being not given over to delusion, not obsessed by delusion, not overcome mentally by delusion, a person does not destroy life, does not steal, does not commit adultery, and does not tell lies, and does not encourage others to do likewise. Will that lead to his long-term well-being and happiness?"

"Yes, Venerable One."

"What do you think, Kalamas? Are these things good or bad?"

"Good, Venerable One."

"Blameworthy or blameless?"

"Blameless, Venerable One."

"Censured or praised by the wise?"

"Praised by the wise, Venerable One."

"Accepted and undertaken, do they lead to a person's long-term well-being and happiness or not?"

"Accepted and undertaken, they lead to a person's long-term well-being and happiness. So it strikes us."

"Therefore Kalamas, do not go based upon oral tradition, etc.....But when you know yourself, 'These things are good, these things are blameless, these things are praised by the wise; when accepted and undertaken, these things lead to well-being and happiness,' then you should live in accordance with them...."

The Four Assurances

…"This noble disciple, Kalamas, whose mind is in this way freed of hatred and ill-will, undefiled and pure, acquires four assurances here and now.

'If there is a world after death and if there are fruits of actions rightly or wrongly done, it is possible with the dissolution of the body after death I will be reborn in another realm, in a blissful state.' This is the first assurance he acquires.

'If there is no world after death if there are no fruits of actions rightly or wrongly done, then in this world here and now, free from hatred, free from ill-will, I maintain myself in happiness, free of trouble.' This is the second assurance he acquires.

'If evil results come to an evil-doer, how then can evil come to me, when I have no thoughts of doing evil to anyone?' This is the third assurance he acquires.

'If evil results do not come to an evil-doer, then I see myself purified in any case.' This is the fourth assurance he acquires.

This noble disciple, Kalamas, whose mind is in this way freed of hatred and ill-will, undefiled and pure, has acquired these four assurances here and now."

"So it is, Blessed One! So it is, Fortunate One. The noble disciple whose mind is in this way freed of hatred and ill-will, undefiled and pure, has acquired these four assurances here and now….Excellent, Venerable One. We go to the Blessed One, to the *dhamma,* and to the sangha of monks for refuge. From today on, let the Blessed One regard us as lay followers who have gone for refuge for life."

CHAPTER V

The Three Marks of Existence

The Buddha taught that there were three essential marks or characteristics of everything that exists: impermanence (*anicca*), insubstantiality or non-self (*annata*), and suffering (*dukkha*). These three apply to all animate forms of life, from the lowliest microbe to the most brilliant human being. Furthermore, the Buddha believed that these three were not simply matters of abstract speculation about reality, but verifiable from our own human experience. Finally, he argued that grasping these three facts about the human condition—understanding reality as it actually is, as opposed to how we would like it to be—is essential for the attainment of wisdom and liberation (SN 22.45, p. 848). Get this part of the Buddha's philosophy right, in other words, and the rest will fall into place.

Impermanence

Everything that we experience in life, the Buddha believed, is subject to impermanence (Pal: *anicca*; San: *anitya*); everything in the universe is subject to flux or change, arises and disappears all the time. This idea is very similar to that developed by the ancient Greek philosopher Heraclitus, who famously observed, "you can't step into the same river twice." The reason that you can't is because the flowing river changes so much it isn't the same river from one moment to the next.

You might think that this characteristic applies only to things that are in motion, like rivers, but in fact it applies to everything in the universe. Everything is subject to the process of change. Call to mind the most majestic mountain that you've ever seen. Mountains certainly appear permanent. Unless some kind of environmental catastrophe has occurred, the mountains that you might have seen as a child might look pretty much the same when you return to see them as an adult—from a distance anyway. But science tells us that things like mountains, in fact, are constantly changing at every moment through the endless process of erosion. Appearances may deceive, but, like the river, you can't step foot on the same mountain twice either.

The key insight of the Buddha can be summed up in the following way: "Impermanent are compounded things, prone to rise and fall" (D 16.6.10, p. 271). Everything in the universe is in a state of flux and change, he teaches us, because all things are compounded, complex, and interconnected: the constitutive elements that comprise these things come together and eventually fall apart. Like rivers and mountains, we too are part of this essential process of change. our body, your mind, your emotions, everything that you think of as "you" is constantly in a state of change, and subject to growth and maturation, but also to decay, degradation, and eventual annihilation. "All that is mine," the Buddha somberly reminds us, "all that is beloved and pleasing to me, will someday be otherwise, will someday be separated from me" (AN: 3.71, p. 686).

This inexorable process of change and interconnectedness is also referred to by the Buddha as "dependent arising" (*patticca samuppada*). So central is this concept to the Buddha's own thought that he described his own awakening in light of it. As you may recall from the previous chapter, upon attaining enlightenment under the Bodhi tree, the Buddha hesitated to share what he experienced with others for fear that they would never be able to grasp what he had to say:

> This *dhamma* that I have attained is profound, hard to see and hard to understand, peaceful and sublime, unattainable by mere reasoning, subtle, to be experienced by the wise. But this generation delights in attachment, takes delight in attachment, rejoices in attachment. It is hard for such

a generation to see this truth, namely [dependent arising] (MN: 26, 19, p. 260).

Dependent arising was and continues to be one of the most difficult concepts in Buddhism for most people to come to grips with, but it is also *the* central concept in Buddhist thought—the cornerstone of the Buddha's entire philosophical system. As he himself succinctly put it, "One who sees [dependent arising] sees the Dhamma; one who sees the Dhamma, sees [dependent arising]" (MN 28.38, p. 284).

So what then is dependent arising? The Buddha himself describes this process in the following way:

> When this exists, that comes to be; with the arising of this, that arises. When this does not exist, that does not come to be; with the cessation of this, that ceases (SN 2.12.37, p. 575).

In a nutshell what the Buddha is describing is actually quite a simple thing to understand, if we just try to grasp things as they are (endlessly changing, dependent upon other things), rather than as we would like them to be (permanent, independent). The idea here is that all things come into existence because of certain conditions present to support their existence. When these conditions change—as they inevitably must—things change. When these conditions disappear—as they also inevitably must—things cease to be. As Stephen Batchelor puts it, dependent arising is the recognition that oneself and the world in which one lives are "fluid, contingent events that spring from fluid contingent events, but that need not have happened" (Bachelor, 131). Simple enough, right? Seeds give rise to plants, but if the seeds don't germinate, there's no plant. Your parents gave birth to you, but what if your parents had been prevented from ever meeting one another? Where would you be then? Or what if they got together with two other people? Would you still be you? You are living and breathing right now because of the presence of certain conditions necessary to support life. But what happens to you when these conditions change or disappear? The answer is that you change or disappear as well.

Non-Self

When we recognize that all things are subject to change and are interdependent, then we also see that all things—including the thing we call ourselves—are insubstantial: they have no abiding nature or essence of their own. They literally have "non-self" (Pal: *annata*; San: *anatman*).

Like dependent arising, the idea of non-self is a very difficult concept for most people to grasp, and probably for good reason. It's difficult for human beings to think of themselves as anything other than permanent, enduring, and abiding selves. When we look in the mirror, it's quite natural to consider the thing being reflected back to us as somehow representing our "true selves"— the being that we've always been and will continue to be, not only in this life but perhaps in some future life as well. If we are a bit philosophical, we may not identify this true self with our bodies per se, because we know that the body is impermanent and subject to decay and dissolution. But we probably still believe that somewhere within our ever-changing bodies is that spiritual (and perhaps eternal) entity that we call ourselves.

In the Western religious traditions, this abiding spiritual self is typically referred to as the soul, and in these traditions, it's the soul, as opposed to the body, that is considered to represent the true "essence" of the human person. But this sort of idea was also common in the Hindu tradition of the Buddha's own time, which argued for the existence of an eternal Self—called *Atman*—that passes from one lifetime to the next. According to the teaching in the Upanishads, it's by realizing this eternal Self within us that ultimate happiness and liberation occurs.

It was this concept of *Atman* that the Buddha flatly rejected when he proposed his own concept of non-self. By claiming that impermanence is not just an essential characteristic of the material world, but also of ourselves, the Buddha came to the logical conclusion that no enduring Self could possibly exist. Instead he argues that all things—including human beings—have the characteristic of "non-self".

To fully understand this idea of non-self, it's vital to grasp the Buddhist concept of the five aggregates (Pal: *kandha*; San: *skandha*). The Buddha maintained that there are five things that comprise what we can refer to as the "conventional self"—those aspects of human identity that people often refer to when they talk about themselves. In essence these are:

- (Material) Form (*rupa*): includes body parts and sense organs.
- Sensations (*vedana*): includes all sensations of the body and which produces pleasant, unpleasant, and neutral feelings.
- Perceptions (*samjna*): recognition of physical objects, thoughts, and ideas.
- Mental Formations (*samskara*): volitional actions (e.g., willing, thinking, imagining) that form one's character in life.
- Consciousness (*vijnana*): mental awareness and self-awareness (awareness of ourselves as thinking subjects

These five constitute on an experiential level all the aspects of who we think that we are and all that we identify with when we describe ourselves. The first aggregate—material form or body—comprises physical reality, representing everything that can be grasped through the senses. The remaining four are mental realities.

There are two essential things to keep in mind when discussing the aggregates. First, the aggregates represent all that there is to what we refer to as a "person." They are "an exhaustive analysis of the individual. They are the world for any given being—there is nothing else besides" (Gethin, 136). The other thing to keep in mind is all the aggregates are impermanent. They continually arise and fall just like everything else in the universe. If all that we are is represented by the five aggregates and if each of the five aggregates is impermanent, then it follows that there can be non-self—in the traditional sense at least—among the aggregates.

What the Buddha argues is that if we examine each of the five aggregates objectively, we soon see that each of the five could only be described as *anatta* (not self). Certainly none could be considered self if by that we mean some kind of permanent, enduring, and abiding substance. In the Upanishadic tradition,

Atman is identified with consciousness. But the Buddha rejects even this idea, arguing that consciousness only arises when the six senses—eye, ear, nose, tongue, body, and mind—experience a sense object. Even consciousness, therefore, can't be considered a permanent substance.

Instead what we discover when we take the time to examine the five aggregates is an ever changing flow of sensations, perceptions, ideas, volitions, and particular acts of consciousness that seems to uproot the notion of any kind of permanent self. Or as the Buddha puts it, it is impossible to look at any of the elements of the conventional self and say, "This is mine, this I am, this is my self" (MN 22.27).

Suffering

The last mark of existence that the Buddha describes is the inevitable reality of suffering that all sentient beings experience as a natural part of life. The word "suffering" is a bit problematic here, because it seems to suggest some kind of intense despair or agony that some people don't seem to possess. In both Pali and Sanskrit the term that the Buddha actually used to describe this mark of existence is "*dukkha*." Although *dukkha* can be translated as "suffering" in the usual sense, the term is actually a bit broader than this. As the Buddha used it *dukkha* could also mean something more like dissatisfactory, unsatisfying, dis-ease, dis-comfort, or stress.

To understand what the Buddha meant by *dukkha*, it is helpful to have the image of a chariot in mind, which is where the origin of the term *dukkha* was derived. The term "*du*" means "bad" (as opposed to "*su*" or good). "*Kha*" refers to the axle hole in a chariot. The term dukkha, then, literally refers to a poorly fitting axle hole that makes one's ride in a chariot bumpy and uncomfortable.

If you think about it this way, life indeed can be described as bumpy, jolting, and unsettling for even those who seem to have it all. For the Buddha, *dukkha* is universal and inescapable. Anyone who has ever lived in the past, anyone who is currently living, and anyone who will ever live in the future experiences *dukkha* in one form or another as part of the ordinary course of life. The reason for this is connected to what we've already discussed—the reality of impermanence. Even the most incredible pleasures and profound enjoyments of life are impermanent: they simply can't be counted on to provide lasting happiness. But part of our human nature is to want the good things we experience in life to go on forever. We delude ourselves into thinking that our pleasures are self-sustaining, that those we love will always be with us, and that we ourselves will be around forever in one form or another.

But if all things are impermanent by their very nature, then nothing we experience in life can be counted on completely. By placing so much reliance on people and things which are essentially unreliable, suffering inevitably arises. We may be able to delude ourselves for a time that the things we love in life will remain as they are forever, but such delusion can't last in the face of reality of impermanence. And so our own selfish delusions become the very source of our misery in life.

In accepting the reality of *dukkha* as an essential feature of existence, the Buddha forces us to recognize that there is a tragic— or at least unpleasant—aspect of life that many us of would prefer not to have to face. If this were the end of the story, Buddhism would probably have gone down in history as the most depressing philosophy of life ever conceived.

Fortunately, the Buddha was an eminently practical thinker. If there is suffering, then he was also convinced that there must also be a way out of suffering. Far from being a pessimist about human existence, the Buddha was one of history's greatest optimists. Not only did he argue that there was a way to escape from suffering, but, as we'll see, he believed that way was completely within our own hands at all times.

READING THE SOURCES

~~~

Impermanence and the Non-Self
[Anatta-lakkhana Sutta]

Thus have I heard.

On one occasion, the Blessed One was residing near Varanasi at the Deer Park at Isipatana. There the Blessed One addressed the group of five monks: "(Material) form (*rupa*), monks, is not the self. If form were the self, this form would not be subject to disease, and we should be able to say: 'Let my form be like this, let my form not be like this.' But since form is not the self, therefore form is subject to disease, and we are not able to say: 'Let my form be like this, let my form not be like this.'"

"Sensations (*vedana*), monks, are not the self....Perceptions (*semjna*) are not the self....Mental formations (*samskara*) are not the self....Consciousness (*vijnana*) is not the self....etc."

"Now what do you think, monks, is the body permanent or impermanent?"

"It is impermanent, Venerable One."

"And that which is impermanent, does that cause suffering or joy?"

"It causes suffering, Venerable One."

"And that which is impermanent, which causes suffering, and which is subject to change, is it possible to regard that in this way: 'This is mine, this is me, this is my self?'"

"No, Venerable One."

"Are sensations permanent or impermanent?...Are perceptions permanent or impermanent?...Are mental formations permanent or impermanent?...Is consciousness permanent or imperma-

---

Alt Trans: SN 22.59, pp. 901-903.

nent?..."

"Impermanent, Venerable One"

"Therefore, monks, whatever form—whether arising in the past, future, or present, whether interior or exterior, whether gross or subtle, whether inferior or superior, whether distant or near—all that form should be considered by those with right understanding as not mine, not me, not my self."

"Whatever sensations....Whatever perceptions....Whatever mental formations....Whatever consciousness—whether arising in the past, future, or present, whether interior or exterior, whether gross or subtle, whether inferior or superior, whether distant or near—all [these] should be considered by those with right understanding as not mine, not me, not my self."

"Recognizing this, monks, a noble hearer of the truth becomes disenchanted with form, with sensations, with perceptions, with mental formations, and with consciousness. Becoming disenchanted [with all that], he detaches himself from passion; by detaching himself from passion he is liberated; when liberated, there comes the knowledge that he is liberated. And he grasps that birth is ended, that holiness is completed, that task is fulfilled, and that there is no further return to any state of becoming."

This is what the Blessed One said. The five monks were delighted, and rejoiced at the words of the Blessed One. And while this discourse was being spoken, the minds of the five monks became liberated by relinquishing their attachments.

There is No Self
[From the Milindapanha]

The text records the meeting between the Buddhist monk Nagasena and the Bactrian Greek King Milinda (Menander). Though this text is not part of the Pali Canon, it is recognized as adhering to the "same doctrine and discipline...as that propounded in the Pali Canon" (Mendis, 10).

"The Question of King Milinda" (*Milindapañha*). Trans. T. W. Rhys Davids. *Sacred Books of the East.* Vol. 35. Oxford: Clarendon Press, 1890. Translation updated.

King Milinda approached the venerable Nagasena, greeted him respectfully, and sat down beside him. Nagasena returned the greeting, delighting King Milinda. Then King Milinda spoke to the venerable Nagasena: "How is your reverence known? What is your name, Venerable one?"

"Your majesty, I am called Nagasena, my fellow-monks address me as Nagasena: but whether parents give one the name Nagasena, or Surasena, or Virasena, or Sihasena, it is, nevertheless only a conventional term, an appellation, a convenient designation, a mere name, this Nagasena, for there is no self here to be found."

Then King Milinda the king said, "Listen to me, you five hundred Greeks, and you eighty thousand monks! Nagasena here says that 'there is no self here to be found.' Is it reasonable for me to assent to what he says?"

Then turning to Nagasena, he said, "Venerable Nagasena, if there is no self to be found, who is it then gives you monks your robes, food, lodgings, and medicine for the sick? Who is it makes use of these things? Who is it keeps the precepts? Who is it applies himself to meditation? Who is it realizes the Paths, the Fruits, and Nirvana? Who is it destroys life? Who is it takes what is not given him? Who is it commits immorality? Who is it tells lies? Who is it drinks intoxicating liquor? Who is it commits the five crimes that bring immediate retribution. In that case, there is no good; there is no evil. There is no one who does or causes to be done good or evil deeds. Neither good nor evil deeds can have any fruit or result. Venerable Nagasena, if he who kills a monk does not exist, then he does not actually take a life; and it is also true that you, Venerable Nagasena, have no teacher, preceptor, or ordination. When you say, 'My fellow-monks, your majesty, address me as Nagasena,' what then is this Nagasena? Please Venerable One, is the hair of the head Nagasena?"

"Certainly not, your majesty."

"Is the hair of the body Nagasena?"

"Certainly not, your majesty."

"Are nails...teeth, skin, flesh, sinews, bones, marrow of the bones, kidneys, heart, liver, membranes, spleen, lungs, intestines, mesentery, stomach, feces, bile, pus, blood, sweat, fat, tears, lymph, saliva, snot, synovial fluid, urine, brain of the head Nagasena?"

"Certainly not, your majesty."

"Is material form Nagasena?"

"Certainly not, your majesty."

"Is sensation...perception...psychic constructions...consciousness Nagasena?"

"Certainly not, your majesty."

"Are then material form sensation, perception, the psychic constructions, and consciousness unitedly, which is Nagasena?"

"Certainly not, your majesty."

"Is there something else, besides material form, sensation, perception, the psychic constructions, and consciousness, which is Nagasena?"

"Certainly not, your majesty."

"Venerable One, although I question you very closely, I fail to discover any Nagasena. It would seem that Nagasena is a mere empty sound. What Nagasena is there here? Venerable One, you speak a falsehood, you utter a lie when you claim that there is no Nagasena."

Then the Venerable Nagasena replied to King Milinda in the following way: "Your majesty,...tell me, did you come here on foot or in a chariot?"

"Venerable One, I do not travel on foot; I came in a chariot."

"Your majesty, if you came in a chariot, tell me about the chariot. Your majesty, is the pole the chariot?"

"Certainly not, Venerable One."

"Is the axle the chariot?"

"Certainly not, Venerable One."

"Are the wheels the chariot?"

"No, truly, Venerable One."

"Is the chariot-body the chariot?...Is the banner-staff the chariot?"..."Is the yoke the chariot?"..."Are the reins the chariot?"..."Is the goading-stick the chariot?"

"Certainly not, Venerable One."

"Your majesty, are pole, axle, wheels, chariot-body, banner-staff, yoke, reins, and goad unitedly the chariot?"

"Certainly not, Venerable One."

"Is there something else, your majesty, besides pole; axle, wheels, chariot-body, banner-staff, yoke, reins, and goad which is the chariot?"

"Certainly not, Venerable One."

"Your majesty, although I question you very closely, I fail to discover any chariot. Truly now, your majesty, the word chariot is a mere empty sound. What chariot is there here? Your majesty, you speak a falsehood, a lie: there is no chariot. Your majesty, you are the chief king in all the continent of India. Of whom are you afraid that you speak a lie? Listen to me, you five hundred Greeks, and you eighty thousand monks! King Milinda here says, 'I came in a chariot;' and being requested, 'Your majesty, if you came in a chariot, tell me about the chariot,' he fails to produce any chariot. Is it reasonable, I ask, for me to assent to what he says?"

Hearing this, the five hundred Greeks applauded the venerable Nagasena and said to King Milinda, "Now, your majesty, answer, if you can."

Then King Milinda said to venerable Nagasena, "Venerable Nagasena, what I said was not false: the word 'chariot' is only a conventional term, appellation, convenient designation, and name for pole, axle, wheels, chariot-body, and banner-staff."

"Your majesty, you understand completely what a chariot is. And exactly the same thing is true with respect to me. Nagasena is only a coventional term, appellation, convenient designation, mere name for the hair of my head, hair of my body . . . brain of the head, form, sensation, perception, the psychic constructions, and consciousness. But in the absolute sense there is no self to be found here. As the priestess Vajira said in the presence of The Blessed One:—

Just as the word of "chariot"
simply refers to an assembly of parts
So, when the aggregates are present,
We use the phrase, "A living being."

"It is wonderful, Venerable Nagasena! It is marvelous, Nagasena! The answers that you have given to these questions are brilliant and highly illuminating! If The Buddha were alive, he would applaud...."

Kisa-Gotami and the Mustard Seed
[Therigetha 10.1]

Gotami was born at Savatthi, into a poor family. Because her body was so skinny, she was called Skinny Gotami. And when she was married, she was treated badly by her husband's family, who regarded her as a daughter of a nobody. It was only when she gave birth to a son that at last people began to treat her with some respect. However, just when the boy was old enough to run about and play, he suddenly became ill and died. And remembering how she had been treated before her son was born, she became crazy with sorrow, [and refused to believe that he was dead]. So she took the dead corpse on her hip and went from door to door, saying, "Give me medicine for my child." People turned away with contempt, saying "Medicine! What's the use?" But she could not grasp what they were saying.

However, one of her neighbors, wiser than the rest, understood that her mind was disturbed with grief for her child...and said, "Dear woman, why don't you go to the Buddha, and ask him for medicine to give your child." So she went to the monastery at the time of the teaching of the *dhamma*, and said: "Blessed One, give me medicine for my child!" The Master, seeing the promise in her, said: "Go, enter the town, and at any house that has not experienced any death, ask those in that household to give you a mustard-seed."

"Very well, lord!" she replied, with her mind relieved. Going to the first house in the town, she said, "If no one has ever died in this house, please let me take a mustard seed." But the woman of the house said, "Who can even begin to count how many have died in this very house."

"Then keep the seed," replied Gotami, "for of what use is it to me."

So she went on to a second and a third house, until at last, thanks to the power of the Buddha, her madness left her and her

Davids, C.A.F. Rhys and Norman, K.R., trans. *Psalms of the Early Buddhists.* Vol. 1: *Psalms of the Sisters.* London: Pali Text Society, 1909. Translation updated.

right mind was restored. Then she thought to herself, "This will be the way it is in the entire town. The Blessed One had foreseen this out of compassion for me." Her mind elevated by this, she left town and laid her child in the burial ground. And then she proclaimed:

> It is not just true for a single village or city,
> nor is it just true for an individual family
> but for the entire worlds of men and gods,
> this is the Law: All is impermanent!

Saying this, she went to the Master. And he said, "Gotami, have you gotten some mustard seed?" And she replied, "The work of the mustard seed is finished and you have restored me."

Then the Master uttered these words:

> A person whose mind clings intemperately
> to children or possessions,
> is swept away like the death that comes
> to a sleepy village in a great flood.

When he had spoken, she was confirmed in the fruit of the first stream-entry and asked for ordination.

CHAPTER VI

The Four Noble Truths

According to tradition, following his enlightenment under the Bodhi tree, the awakened Siddhattha Gotama sought out his former ascetic companions in order to convey to them what he had experienced. When he caught up with them at the Deer Park in Sarnath, he taught what would become known as the Four Noble Truths—what many consider to be the heart of the Buddha's teaching. These insights would later be recorded in the *Dhammacakkappavattana Sutta* (Discourse on Setting the Wheel of the *Dhamma* in Motion). If there's one text that could be called essential reading for all Buddhists, this would certainly be it.

As important as this text is in the Buddhist cannon, the Buddha's explication of the famed Four Noble Truths is condensed into four relatively short verses:

Now this, [monks], is the noble truth of suffering: birth is suffering, aging is suffering, illness is suffering, death is suffering; union with what is displeasing is suffering; separation from what is pleasing is suffering; not to get what one wants is suffering; in brief, the five aggregates subject to clinging are suffering.

Now this, [monks], is the noble truth of the origin of suffering: it is this craving which leads to renewed existence, accompanied by delight and lust, seeking delight here and there; that is, craving for sensual pleasures, craving for [becoming], craving for [non-becoming].

Now this, [monks], is the noble truth of the cessation of suffering: it is the remainderless fading away and cessa-

tion of that same craving, the giving up and relinquishing
of it, freedom from it, nonreliance on it.

Now this, [monks], is the noble truth of the way leading to the cessation of suffering: it is this Noble Eightfold
Path; that is, right view, right intention, right speech, right
action, right livelihood, right effort, right mindfulness,
right concentration (SN 56.11.p. 1844).

Entire books have been written about the Four Noble Truths, but
in the *Dhammacakkappavattana Sutta* the details of the Buddha's
first teachings on the subject are amazingly sketchy, to say the
least. And yet within this brief outline of his thought is contained
the essence of the Buddha's teaching.

The term *ariya sacca* (San: *arya satya*) that is used in the sutta
is usually translated as "noble truths." Literally, the term "*sacca*"
means "real," "true," or "true reality," and the term "*ariya*" means
"noble ones" (i.e., those who have achieved enlightenment). *Ariya sacca* therefore literally means "the truths of the noble ones."
In other words, the Four Noble Truths articulated by the Buddha
in this sutta should be understood as basic facts about our human
experience that can be grasped by anyone who follows the *dhamma*. These four "truths" should not be understood as propositions
to be assented to as a matter of faith, but convey important truths
about reality itself. They are also universal truths, because they
apply to all of us regardless of our station in life.

In expressing these four truths the Buddha used what many
have described as a medical model of analysis. If *dukkha* could be
compared to a sickness and the Buddha a spiritual physician, then
the four noble truths could be compared with a program of medical treatment. In attempting to diagnose an illness, a physician
would (1) define the nature of the illness, (2) identify the cause of
the illness, (3) make a prognosis as to whether the illness could
be successfully treated or not, and finally, (4) prescribe a cure that
would lead the patient to good health.

Thus, the Four Noble Truths, as they are often expressed, are:

1. There is suffering,
2. There is a cause of suffering,
3. There is the cessation of suffering,

4. There is the path leading to the cessation of suffering—the Eightfold Path.

The First Noble Truth: There is Suffering

In the previous chapter, we briefly explored the Buddha's understanding of *dukkha*. Now it's time to delve a bit deeper into this phenomenon in order to better understand why he believed suffering to be inevitable. The Buddha has been called a pessimist for beginning his philosophy by focusing on the reality of human suffering. In fact he was a consummate realist. If we remember the medical model described above, it makes perfect sense to begin any sort of program of treatment with a clear understanding of the nature of the illness to be treated. After all, unless we first understand what ails us, there's no possibility for any kind of legitimate cure.

And what ails every human being who ever lived and who ever will live is *dukkha*—suffering, dis-ease, dissatisfaction. Call it what you will, the reality of *dukkha* is such that the lives of all human beings are inevitably going to be bumpy and distressing at one point or another (Remember the image of the poorly fitting axle hole?).

The Buddha's investigation of the nature of suffering led him to three distinct kinds of suffering that human beings experience during the course of their lives:

(1) Suffering as a Result of Painful Experience [or Ordinary Suffering] (*dukkha dukkha*). It's hard to deny that there are many aspects of our lives that are painful. The examples that the Buddha uses—birth, old age, illness, and death—are indeed painful and ultimately unavoidable. The pain that we experience in life, however, does not simply include physical pain (headaches, kidney stones), but mental pain as well (the death of a loved one, the loss of a job). It's also important to note that the Buddha didn't believe that pain necessarily gives rise to suffering, but rather it's the way we respond to pain that causes suffering. For example, two people can have the same sort of intense knee pain, but one suffers while the other doesn't, because the former treats her pain with aversion and longs for her old pain-free life back, while the latter accepts her condition and tries to deal with it as best she

can. As the old saying goes: "pain is unavoidable; suffering is optional."

(2) Suffering as a Result of Change (*viparinama dukkha*). Suffering can also be caused by the changing circumstances in our lives and our unskillful reactions to them. We suffer because we desire things to remain as we want them to be—especially when things are going well. But even when life is going completely our way, our pleasure is always tainted by the realization that what we enjoy most in life can disappear at any time. In fact, given the reality of impermanence (*annica*), we can be well assured that everything we love in life will eventually be snatched away. This realization inevitably creates a certain amount of insecurity.

(3) Suffering as a Result of Conditioned Existence *(sankhara-dukkha)*. As you may recall, before he died, the Buddha reminded his followers that all conditioned things are impermanent, subject to change. Given the inevitability of change in our lives, a self-reflective person will eventually experience a certain amount of discontent, not from any specific negative experiences in life (e.g., the break-up of a marriage), but from a deeper nagging unease about life itself—that the very transience of our existence makes life seem fundamentally dissatisfying and even meaningless. In Western philosophy the term given to this deep feeling of uneasiness about life itself is called "*angst*"—anxiety, despair, or dread about the seeming pointlessness of life itself.

The Buddha didn't think that the reality of human suffering was something that needed to be demonstrated, since human experience itself bears out the truth of human suffering of the different kinds described above. When he states, "There is suffering," he means this as an axiomatic—or self-evident—truth. It's important to understand, however, that he is most certainly *not* saying that happiness cannot be found at all in life; simply that whatever happiness we attain in this life is fleeting at best, and hence a source of immense dissatisfaction for human beings.

The Second Noble Truth: There is a Cause of Suffering

Things like sickness, old age, pain and death are an inevitable part of any human life and we can't do anything to change that. But we've also seen that painful conditions and changing circumstances need not necessarily lead to suffering. So what then is the real cause of suffering? The answer for the Buddha is that *tanha* causes suffering. This term is often inaccurately translated as "desire." It's sometimes claimed that Buddha said that desire itself was the cause of our suffering in life. But this is ridiculous. The desire for an ice cream cone on a hot day or the desire to be loved doesn't necessarily cause suffering. Desire is a part of life and we can't do without it. If we had no desire for life itself, we wouldn't go on living; if we had no desire for enlightenment, we would never become liberated. So the problem can't be with desire *per se*.

The term "*tanha*" literally means "thirst." The type of desire that the Buddha is talking about that leads to suffering, therefore, is better translated as "craving"—a kind of intense and obsessive desire that arises out of ignorance. In the *Dhammacakkappavattana Sutta* he goes on to describe three types of craving that lead to suffering:

(1) Craving for Sense Pleasure (*kama tanha*). This is the easiest type of the desire to understand because most of us have experienced it in one form or another. We've all tried to find excitement and delight in objects of the senses—a wonderful meal, a new pair of shoes, the latest technological gadget, etc. The problem is that these objects by their very nature are impermanent. Any attempt to find lasting happiness in them, therefore, can only lead to frustration. And the frustration we experience in pursuing objects of the senses in turn fuels the desire for more sensual pleasures—the craving for ever new experiences and objects to delight us.

(2) Craving for Becoming (*bhava tanha*). This kind of craving is the desire to become something other than one is. If I'm middle class, I might desire to become wealthy; if I'm physically unprepossessing, I might want to become more attractive. Not all craving for becoming is bad: for example, a person may want to become a doctor in order to heal the sick, or an enlightened being in order to help alleviate the suffering of others. These are fine and noble ambitions. Suffering arises, however, when we think achieving our goals in life will necessarily make us happy, and

this is not necessarily going to be the case.

(3) Craving for Non-Becoming (*vibhava tanha*): On a basic level, craving for non-becoming represents dissatisfaction with something specific in one's life that causes displeasure and the desire to get rid of it. It could be as simple as wanting to be freed of the pimples on your face or trying to get rid of the painful emotions that are an inevitable part of life. This form of craving, though, can take on a more existential form when the thing that one wishes to be rid of is one's very self. A life in pursuit of endless sense pleasures for some people can become so tedious that life itself becomes the problem. One tries to escape from one's disenchantment for life by indulging in drugs and alcohol or—in extreme cases—trying to put an end to life itself.

The problem with craving in all of its forms is that it leads to attachment, clinging, possessiveness—the desire for things to be the way we want them to be instead of the way they are. As long as we have attachments to things that are inherently unstable and ever-changing, we will inevitably experience suffering.

The Third Noble Truth: There is the Cessation of Suffering

In the first two noble truths the Buddha teaches us that life contains suffering and that the cause of suffering is craving. The next step in his diagnosis of the problem of suffering is to determine whether this "sickness" can in fact be cured. If it can't, then what we are left with is the worst sort of nihilism imaginable: The Buddha would be telling us that suffering is inevitable but there's no hope of escape from it. In that case, we'd probably be better off just following our craving for non-becoming and end our lives right now. Fortunately, the prognosis for overcoming our suffering is a fairly positive one.

If craving is the cause of suffering, then it follows that the cessation of suffering comes when we let go of our craving. This state of cessation of both craving and suffering is known in Buddhism as *Nibbāna* (San: *Nirvāna*). This might be surprising, because some people believe that "nirvana"—as it's commonly understood, anyway—refers to the experience of spiritual bliss in some otherworldly state. But in the Third Noble Truth what the Buddha reveals is that *Nibbāna* is nothing other than being in a state of cessation and that this state is possible here and now. "When one abides uninflamed by lust," he says, "...one's craving...is abandoned. One's bodily and mental torments are abandoned, one's bodily and mental fevers are abandoned and one experiences bodily and mental pleasure" (MN 149.9, p. 1138).

We'll have more to say about *Nibbāna*, which is the ultimate goal of the Buddhist path, in just a bit. First we need to talk about the specific plan the Buddha prescribes to ultimately cure our suffering—the Noble Eightfold Path.

The Fourth Noble Truth: There is the Path Leading to the Cessation of Suffering—The Noble Eightfold Path

Referring to the Buddha's medical model of analysis again, if the "sickness" of suffering can indeed be cured, as the Buddha optimistically maintains in the Third Noble Truth, then the next step must be to lay out a detailed treatment plan to achieve this end. And this plan is nothing other than the Noble Eightfold Path: right understanding, right intention, right speech, right action, right livelihood, right effort, right mindfulness, and right concentration.

READING THE SOURCES

―⁓―

Setting the Wheel of the Dhamma in Motion
[Dhammacakkappavattana Sutta]

Thus have I heard.
   On one occasion the Blessed One was residing at Varana-si at the Deer Park at Isipatana. There he addressed the five ascetics:

The Middle Path

Monks, there are two extremes that ought not to be indulged in by one who has left the life of a householder. What are these two? One is the way of indulgence to sense pleasure, which is crude, low, vulgar, unworthy and unprofitable. The other is the way of self-mortification, which is painful, unworthy, and unprofitable too.

   Avoiding both these extremes, the *Tathagata* has realized the Middle Path. This path gives vision and knowledge, and leads to calm, to insight, to awakening, and to *Nibbāna*.

The Four Noble Truths and the Eightfold Path

And what is this Middle Path realized by the *Tathagata* that gives vision and knowledge, and leads to calm, to insight, to awakening, and to *Nibbāna*? It is simply the Noble Eightfold Path—namely, right view, right intention, right speech, right action, right livelihood, right effort, right mindfulness, and right concentration. This is the Middle Path realized by the *Tathagata* that gives vision

---

Alt Trans: SN 56.11, pp. 1843-1847

and knowledge, and leads to calm, to insight, to awakening, and to *Nibbāna.*

This is the noble truth of suffering (*dukkha*): Birth is suffering; aging is suffering; sickness is suffering; death is suffering; sorrow, lamentation, pain, distress, and despair are suffering; dealing with what is unpleasant is suffering; separation from the pleasant is suffering; not getting what one wants is suffering—in short, the five aggregates subject to grasping are suffering.

This is the noble truth of the cause of suffering: It is the craving (*tanha*) that produces rebirth accompanied by passion and greed, and delighting in this and that—in short, the craving for sense pleasure, the craving for becoming, and the craving for non-becoming.

This is the noble truth of the cessation of suffering: It is the total cessation of craving—the renunciation, relinquishment, releasing, and letting go of that craving.

This is the noble truth of the path leading to the cessation of suffering: It is the Noble Eightfold Path—namely, right view, right intention, right speech, right action, right livelihood, right effort, right mindfulness, and right concentration.

The Realization of the Dhamma by the Buddha

This is the noble truth of suffering. This was the vision, the insight, the wisdom, the science, the illumination that arose within me, regarding ideas never heard before....This noble truth of suffering has been fully comprehended.

This is the noble truth of the cause of suffering. This was the vision, the insight, the wisdom, the science, the illumination that arose within me, regarding ideas never heard before....This noble truth of the cause of suffering has been abandoned.

This is the noble truth of the cessation of suffering....This was the vision, the insight, the wisdom, the science, the illumination that arose within me, regarding ideas never heard before....This noble truth of the cessation of suffering has been realized.

This is the noble truth of the path leading to the cessation of suffering....This was the vision, the insight, the wisdom, the science, the illumination that arose within me, regarding ideas never heard before....This noble truth of the path leading to the cessation of suffering has been realized.

As long as my knowledge and vision of things as they actually are...was not completely purified, I could not claim to have realized [full enlightenment]....But once my knowledge and vision of things as they actually are...became purified...then I did claim to have realized [full enlightenment]. Knowledge and vision arose within me: I have finally been released. This birth is my last. Now there will be no more rebirth.

The Reception of the Buddha's Teaching

This is what the Blessed One said. The five ascetics were delighted and rejoiced in his words. While his discourse was being delivered, there arose in the Venerable Kondanna, the dust-free, stainless vision of the *dhamma* and he said: "Whatever is subject to arising is subject to ceasing."

When the Blessed One set in motion the wheel of the *dhamma*, the earth gods proclaimed, "At Varanasi at the Deer Park at Isipatana, the Blessed One has set in motion the unparalleled wheel of the *dhamma*, which cannot be stopped by monk,...or gods, or anyone in the world." On hearing the earth gods' cry, all the gods above [raised the same cry]....

Then the Blessed One exclaimed: "Kondanna knows; he really knows." And this is how the Venerable Kondanna got the name "Anna-Kondanna"—Kondanna who knows.

Craving

The Perils of Craving
[The Dhammapada]

334. The craving (*tanha*) of a thoughtless man grows like a creeping vine. He runs around here and there, like a monkey seeking fruit in the forest.

Alt Trans: DMP, 184-187.

335. Whoever is overcome by this fierce craving in this world finds that his sufferings increase like [grass after the rains].

336. Whoever overcomes this fierce craving in this world is difficult to be conquered. Sufferings fall off from him, like water-drops from a lotus leaf.

337. This I will say to all gathered here: Dig up the root of craving, like one in search of a fragrant root digs out the grass above, so that Mara (the tempter) may not crush you again and again, as the stream crushes the reeds.

338. Just as a cut down tree will grow again as long as its root is sound and firm, so will suffering return again and again if your tendency towards craving is not rooted out.

339. The misguided man, whose craving for pleasure is overwhelming…, will be carried off by the waves that are his own desires fixated on passion.

340. The currents run in all directions, and the creeping vine (of passion), having sprung up, becomes established. When you see that creeper spring up, cut its roots by means of wisdom.

341. Seeking extravagant and luxurious delights, a man becomes sunken in lust and keen on pleasure, and thus undergoes birth and decay (again and again).

342. Men driven on by craving run about like hunted hares. Held in fetters and bonds, they undergo lasting suffering over and over.

343. Men driven on by craving run about like hunted hares. Therefore [one] who desires to be free of passion, should drive out their craving.

344. When a man who has escaped from the forest of lust has been drawn back into that forest, then free from the forest as he is, he runs right back into it. Look at him; once free, he has returned to his bondage.

345. Wise people do not call a manacle strong which is made of iron, wood or hemp. A far stronger manacle is the attachment to jewels and rings, children and wives.

346. That manacle that wise people call strong is one that drags one downward—one that feels loose, but which is actually is very difficult to break. When at last one breaks this manacle, he renounces the world, abandoning sensual pleasures.

347. Those who are slaves to passion, fall back into the swirling stream of desires, as a spider runs down a web which he has made himself. When the wise have cut this off, they become free of longing and leave all suffering behind.

348. Let go of your cravings of the future; let go of your cravings of the past; let go of your cravings of the present. Cross over to the opposite shore of existence. If your mind becomes free, you will not enter again into birth and death.

349. When a man is tossed above by his own troubled thoughts and is filled with passion, fixated on what is enticing, his craving steadily grows. Such a man makes his manacles strong indeed.

350. The man who delights in calming his thoughts, mindfully reflecting on the impurities of the bodies, will put an end to craving and cut the bonds of Mara.

351. He who has reached this goal, and is without fear, craving or moral blemish, has plucked out the thorns of existence. This will be his last body.

352. He who is without craving and attachment, an expert in the study of texts and their interpretation, he is indeed, the bearer of his last body and is called the sage, the great man.

353. I am the conqueror of all, I am the knower of all. But unattached am I to all that is conquered and known, Through the destruction of craving, I am free. Having achieved realization myself, whom shall I call my teacher?

354. The gift of the *dhamma* exceeds all gifts; the sweetness of the *dhamma* exceeds all sweetness; the delight in the *dhamma* exceeds all delights; the extinction of craving overcomes all suffering.

355. Riches destroy the foolish, yet not those who seek the other shore. The fool by his craving for riches destroys himself, as if he were destroying his own enemy.

356. Fields are damaged by weeds; mankind is damaged by passion. Therefore what is offered to those free of passion bears great fruit.

357. Fields are damaged by weeds; mankind is damaged by hatred. Therefore what is offered to those free of hatred bears great fruit.

358. Fields are damaged by weeds; mankind is damaged by

delusion. Therefore what is offered to those free of delusion bears great fruit.

359. Fields are damaged by weeds, mankind is damaged by craving. Therefore a gift bestowed on those who are free from craving brings great reward.

Craving as the Cause of Suffing
[Mahadukkakkhandha Sutta]

It is due to craving...that kings fight against kings, nobles against nobles, brahmins against brahmins, householders against householders, mother against child, child against mother, father against son, son against father, brother against brother, sister against sister, brother against sister, sister against brother, friend against friend. And then, having fallen into quarrels, contention, and strife, they attack one another using fists, weapons of the earth, sticks, and knives, leading to death or deadly suffering.....

Again, due to craving...people take up shields and swords and wear bows and arrows. They charge into battle, with arrows and spears flying and swords hacking. And here they suffer death or deadly suffering....

Again, due to craving....people break into houses, carry off plunder, engage in burglary, ambush one another, and commit adultery. Upon being arrested by authorities, they are punished in many different ways—by being whipped, beaten, and clubbed. They have their hands cut off, their feet cut off, their hands and feet cut off, their ears cut off, their noses cut off, their ears and noses cut off....

Again, due to craving...people engage in bodily, verbal and mental misconduct. Having engaged in bodily, verbal, and mental misconduct, they experience a mass of suffering in future states.... These perils that await one in future states are due to craving... [and] have craving as their cause.

Alt Trans: MN 13.14-15, p. 182

The Fire Sermon
[Adittapariyaya Sutta]

I have heard that one occasion the Blessed One was staying at Gaya, at Gaya Head, with 1000 monks. There he addressed the monks:

"Monks, all things are on fire. And what is on fire?

The eye is on fire; forms are on fire; eye-consciousness is on fire; impressions received by the eye are on fire; and whatever sensation, pleasant, unpleasant, or indifferent, originates in dependence on impressions received by the eye, that also is on fire.

And with what are these on fire?

With the fire of passion, with the fire of hatred, with the fire of delusion; with birth, old age, death, sorrow, lamentation, misery, grief, and despair are they on fire.

The ear is on fire. Sounds are on fire....The nose is on fire. Smells are on fire....The tongue is on fire; tastes are on fire.... The body is on fire; tactile sensations are on fire....The mind is on fire; ideas are on fire. Mind-consciousness is on fire; impressions received by the mind are on fire; and whatever sensation, pleasant, unpleasant, or indifferent, originates in dependence on impressions received by the mind, that also is on fire.

And with what are these on fire?

They are on fire with the fire of passion, with the fire of hatred, with the fire of infatuation; with birth, old age, death, sorrow, lamentation, misery, grief, and despair they are on fire.

Seeing this, O monks, the learned and noble disciple grows disenchanted with the eye, grows disenchanted with forms, grows disenchanted with eye-consciousness, grows disenchanted with impressions received by the eye; and he grows disenchanted with whatever sensation, pleasant, unpleasant, or indifferent, originates in dependence on impressions received by the eye.

Alt Trans: SN 35.28, p. 1143.

He grows disenchanted with the ear. He grows disenchanted with sounds....He grows disenchanted with the nose. He grows disenchanted with smells....He grows disenchanted with the tongue. He grows disenchanted with tastes. He grows disenchanted with the body. He grows disenchanted with tactile sensations.... he grows disenchanted with the mind. He grows disenchanted with ideas. He grows disenchanted with mind-consciousness. He grows disenchanted with the impressions received by the mind; and whatever sensation, pleasant, unpleasant, or indifferent, originates in dependence on impressions received by the mind, for this also he grows disenchanted.

And, having become disenchanted, he loses his attachment for these things, and by becoming detached he becomes free, and when he is free he becomes aware that he is free; and he knows that rebirth is exhausted, that he, has lived the holy life, that he has done what it behooved him to do, and that there is nothing more for this world."

This is what the Blessed One said. And while this exposition was being delivered, the minds of the thousand monks became free from their attachments....

Daibutsu Buddha (Kamakura, Japan, 13th century)

CHAPTER VII

The Eightfold Path

The Buddha was convinced that, while suffering (*dukka*) is a pervasive feature of the human experience, there must also be a way out of suffering. The plan that he devised for this liberation from suffering has come to be known as the "Noble Eightfold Path."

Far from thinking that he himself was the originator of this action plan for liberation, the Buddha describes this as an "ancient path" that he rediscovered upon his awakening:

> …[Monks], I saw the ancient path, the ancient road travelled by the Perfectly Enlightened Ones of the past. And what is that ancient path, that ancient road? It is just this Noble Eightfold Path: right view, right intention, right speech, right action, right livelihood, right effort, right mindfulness, right concentration. I followed that path and by doing so I have directly known [suffering], its origin, its cessation, and the way leading to its cessation….Having directly known them, I have explained them to the [monks], the nuns, the male lay followers, and the female lay followers. This holy life, [monks], has become successful and prosperous, extended, popular, widespread, well proclaimed among the devas and humans (SN 12.65, p. 603-604)

Indeed, much of what the Buddha prescribes as a treatment plan to end suffering was hardly new at all. The Buddha's Brahmanical predecessors had already argued that things like moral behavior and meditation could lead one to a state of enlightenment. The Buddha's genius was to take practices that were part of the common spiritual currency of his time and (1) fit them into his new understanding of reality and (2) present these practices in a more integrated way than had been attempted before.

Note the Buddha's use of the term "right" in the passage above to describe each of the eight steps along the path. The Pali term is actually "*samma*," which means ideal, wise, or skillful. The term "right," therefore, should not be taken in the sense of a duty or some kind of obligation. Rather, these are steps, which, if put into practice in one's daily life will eventually lead one to *Nibbāna*.

Traditionally, the Eightfold Path is represented by the image of the *Dhamma* Wheel with the eight spokes of the wheel representing the eight divisions of the path the Buddha advises us to follow:

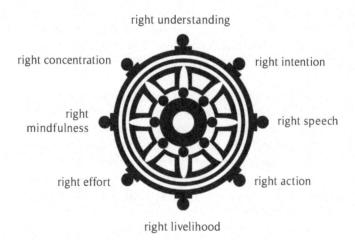

right understanding

right concentration

right intention

right mindfulness

right speech

right effort

right action

right livelihood

Even though the Eightfold Path is represented as a list, this does not mean that the Buddha is suggesting that the eight aspects of the path must necessarily be developed sequentially (for example, starting with right understanding and proceeding to right intention, and so on). As we'll see, although there is a logic to the sequencing of the various divisions of the path, a good way to interpret the term "*samma*" is as something "integral," "whole" or "holistic"—as one path with various components. As Ajahn Sucitto describes it, the Eightfold Path consists of eight interrelated aspects that should be seen as "a mandala of interconnected factors that support and moderate each other" (88). The path can also be seen as a kind of all-encompassing action plan, weaving together the myriad aspects of our inner and outer lives:

> The path of the Buddha is multiple and involves all aspects of our lives. First it has to do with how we view the world and what kind of thoughts we are having. Then it considers how to speak, how to connect with others, how we act and how we live, how we earn our living and sustain our life. Finally, it looks at how we use our energy, how we can be aware and how we can focus. So we start by looking internally, then externally, and then internally again. The Buddha is concerned with the interaction between our inner world and outer world (M. Batchelor, 10).

Since each element of the path reinforces and supports one another, all eight elements of the path should be developed simultaneously to the best of each person's abilities. It's not just enough, therefore, to read books on Buddhism (the "right understanding" aspect of the path), one also needs to practice behaving morally (right speech, right action, right livelihood) and develop a regular meditation practice (right effort, right mindfulness, right concentration). On the other hand, all the meditation in the world won't help us if we have the wrong understanding of reality (right understanding) or the wrong motivation for living our lives (right intention). The all-encompassing nature of the Eightfold Path is also evident from the fact that just about every aspect of the Buddha's teaching as it is revealed throughout the Buddhist suttas in one form or another treats some aspect of this path (Rahula, 45).

There's obviously quite a lot to the Eightfold Path that could provide one with fodder for a lifetime of study. The following explanation aims simply at providing a general overview of each of the eight elements of the Buddha's path to enlightenment. For further information about anything discussed, I encourage you to consult Bhikku Bodi's wonderful text *The Noble Eightfold Path:*

The Way to the End of Suffering.
A traditional way of looking at the Eightfold Path is to see it as a division of three groupings: wisdom, morality, and mental development:

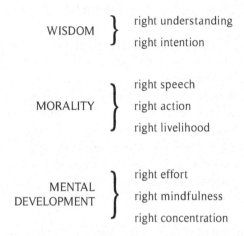

| WISDOM | } | right understanding |
| | | right intention |

MORALITY	}	right speech
		right action
		right livelihood

MENTAL DEVELOPMENT	}	right effort
		right mindfulness
		right concentration

Wisdom

Wisdom (Pal: *pañña*; San: *prajñā*) can be considered a preparatory stage along the Eightfold Path. It involves developing a philosophical understanding of reality that girds and supports the entire structure of the path that the Buddha laid out. The wisdom component of the Eightfold Path involves two elements—right understanding and right intention.

1. Right Understanding (Samma Ditthi)

Right understanding could be called the theoretical element of the path—the other seven elements being more practical in nature, since they involve various sorts of conduct and practices. Right understanding provides one with the correct philosophical understanding of reality as it is developed in three marks of existence and the four noble truths.

There's a good reason why the Buddha placed right understanding first in his discussion of the Eightfold Path. Right understanding functions as a kind of underlying theoretical framework, assuring that, as we proceed through the remaining seven elements of the path we won't be acting out of misunderstanding or delusion.

2. Right Intention (Samma Sankappa)

The Pali term *sankappa* means purpose, resolve, intention, aspiration. Having gained the correct view of reality, the next step along the eightfold path should be to have the correct intentions and motivations in life specifically with regard to the desire to improve ourselves morally and to develop ourselves mentally. For the Buddha such right intention involves renouncing the cravings that cause suffering and actions that cause harm and suffering to others.

This in turn, leads naturally to the next three elements of the path, dealing specifically with ethical behavior.

Morality

Morality or ethical conduct (*sila*) moves us from the inner life of philosophical discernment to the outer world of action and *kamma*. The Buddha viewed right moral behavior as just as important as meditation to attain an untroubled mind. Buddhist morality, however, should not be understood in the Judeo-Christian sense as a set of commandments to be obeyed absolutely, but is more like guiding principles that ought to be followed if we want a life free from suffering. As such, wisdom will always play a large role in determining in any given circumstance how we ought to behave.

Moral action, as it manifests itself in right speech, action, and livelihood, takes the insights that have been developed through the cultivation of wisdom and applies it to the external world. Ethical behavior also becomes an essential pre-condition for mental development. The moral component to the Eightfold Path involves three practices—right speech, right action, and right livelihood.

3. Right Speech (Samma Vaca)

There are four components to right speech:

1. refraining from false speech.
2. refraining from slanderous speech.
3. refraining from harsh speech.
4. refraining from idle chatter (gossip).

In the *Abhaya Sutta* (MN 58, pp. 498-501), the Buddha gives a helpful guideline for determining what sorts of speech acts to avoid. Before we speak, he says, we should reflect on whether our speech is true, beneficial, kind, and timely. If it turns out that what we are about to say is untrue, not beneficial (i.e., a matter of idle speculation), unkind, or untimely (the right words, but at the wrong time or occasion), we would do well, he maintains, to avoid speaking.

4. Right Action (Samma Kammanta)

In general, right action means behaving in a way that would not cause unnecessary harm or suffering to oneself or others. Right action, therefore, includes—but is certainly not limited to—the following:

1. refraining from taking life.
2. refraining from taking what is not given (stealing).
3. refraining from sexual misconduct.

In the *Ambalatthikarahulovada Sutta* (Advice to Rahula), the Buddha provides a method of self-examination of actions of body, speech, and mind by continually reflecting upon them. Concerning right action, specifically, the Buddha advises that before we initiate any action we ask a simple question: "[D]oes this action that I have done with the body lead to my own affliction, or the affliction of others, or the affliction of both." If the answer is yes, it is an unskillful action and we ought not perform it (MN 61, p. 524).

5. Right Livelihood (Samma Ajiva)

Samma ajiva literally means "right way of life." What it means in practice is that one should not seek to earn any kind of living that would cause unnecessary harm or suffering to oneself or others. This path is specifically for laypeople, since Buddha's monks supported themselves by seeking alms. The type of occupations, therefore, that should be avoided by anyone are:

1. trade in weapons (manufacturing or selling any kind of arms)
2. trade in human beings (slave trading)
3. trade in flesh (prostitution)
4. trade in intoxicants (manufacturing or selling any kind of intoxicating drinks or drugs)
5. trade in poisons (manufacturing or selling any kind of substance intended to cause harm)

Mental Development

The final grouping of the eightfold path is sometimes translated as concentration, since the term used in the suttas is "*samadhi*". In one sense this is correct, since concentration is a prerequisite for any kind of Buddhist meditation. On the other hand, the various meditative practices described in the last three paths are broader than the practice *samadhi* as it's traditionally understood. A better translation, therefore, would be something like "mental development" or even simply "meditation." Including right effort, right mindfulness, and right concentration, mental development involves the practices of overcoming the habitual way that the mind operates, enabling it to become unified under our control, and providing the mind with the opportunity to grasp on an intuitive level the true nature of reality.

6. Right Effort (Samma Vayama)

Right effort represents a bridge between the morality and the wisdom branches of the eightfold path. The problem that we often experience when trying to live a moral life is that our ideals can conflict with our actual behavior. For example, it's not so easy simply to decide, "I'm going to avoid gossiping about others from now on." We all know that gossiping is wrong and yet we all do it anyway. What's needed to ensure that we actually can consistently practice behaving correctly is for the mind to be inclined towards skillful ways of acting and disinclined towards the unskillful. As the Buddha puts it, "whatever [one] frequently thinks and ponders on, that will become the inclination of his mind" (MN 19.11, p. 209). This is where right effort comes into play.

Right effort is the conscious and consistent practice to rid oneself of unskillful or unwholesome (*akusala*) states of mind and develop skillful or wholesome (*kusala*) states of mind. Unskillful states are those which arise out the of the three "root poisons" of greed (*lobha*), aversion (*dosa*), and delusion (*moha*), while skillful states arise out of their opposites: non-greed (*alobha*), non-aversion (*adosa*), and non-delusion (*amoha*)—in other words, from generosity, compassionate love, and wisdom.

The practice of right effort involves four aspects—two related to states of mind that have already arisen, and two related to states of mind yet to arise:

1. Preventing unskillful states of mind from arising
2. Abandoning unskillful states of mind that have already arisen
3. Arousing skillful states of mind that have not yet arisen
4. Maintaining skillful states of that have already arisen.

Let's use the example of gossiping again to illustrate how one would prevent an unskillful state of mind from arising: a person who has formed the right intention to live a moral life (right intention), recognizes that gossiping is a harmful practice, and resolves not to gossip again (right speech). At one point or another, a temptation to gossip will arise in the mind. Recognizing this as an unskillful state arising out of aversion, one reflects on the unskillful thought as it arises in the mind without reacting to it until it eventually subsides (as everything in time eventually subsides). No unskillful thought takes root, no unskillful words are uttered.

But repressing unskillful states of mind is not enough; one also needs to work to arouse skillful states. To accomplish this, the Buddha advised the use of a meditative practice aimed at cultivating the positive emotions of loving kindness, compassion, sympathetic joy, and equanimity that have come to be known as the four "divine abodes" (*Brahma-viharas*). To put it simply, opposing states of mind cannot exist together. So if one practices cultivating a mind of loving-kindness, it will be extremely difficult for hatred, for example, to also arise in the mind.

7. Right Concentration (Samma Samadhi)

A second common form of Buddhist meditation practice, as we've already seen, is one that was common throughout India during the time of the Buddha—*samadhi* meditation. *Samadhi* literally means "being firmly put together." The practice involves focusing the mind on some single object of attention—typically the breath—until it achieves a state of concentrated absorption (*jhāna*). At times this "single-pointedness of mind" is spoken of as an end in itself; at other times this state is seen as a preparation for the practice of mindfulness.

Whether *samadhi* is the goal itself or the means to a higher goal, the practice of *samadhi* meditation is one that requires constant effort and practice.

8. Right Mindfulness (Samma Sati)

The reason that right mindfulness is at times discussed last when treating the Eightfold Path is that in some ways it can be seen as a culminating practice in Buddhism. For one thing, the Buddha himself described mindfulness as "the direct path" to *Nibbāna*. It's also the step on the path that leads right back to the first step—right understanding—since the practice of mindfulness leads to an intuitive grasp of the nature of reality that we've understood only conceptually before.

Mindfulness practice involves training in what is known as the Four Foundations of Mindfulness:

1. Mindfulness of the body (*kaya*)
2. Mindfulness sensations (*vedana*)
3. Mindfulness of mind-states (*citta*)
4. Mindfulness of mind-objects (*dhamma*).

The goal of the practice is to developing a mind that is sufficiently alert, unperturbable, and open to experience that it resides equanimously with whatever it experiences and to grasp reality as it is, rather than how we would like it to be.

We'll have more to say about concentration and mindfulness practice when we discuss the Buddha's approach to meditative practice in the next chapter of this text.

READING THE SOURCES

~~~

The Noble Eightfold Path
[Mahasatipatthana Sutta]

And what, monks, is the noble truth of the path leading to the cessation of suffering? It is simply the Noble Eightfold Path—namely, right view, right intention, right speech, right action, right livelihood, right effort, right mindfulness, right concentration.

And what, monks, is right view? It is knowledge of suffering, knowledge of the origin of suffering, knowledge of the cessation of suffering, knowledge of the path leading to the cessation of suffering. This is called right view.

And what, monks, is right intention? It is the aspiration to [live a life] of renunciation [from sensual craving] and freedom from ill-will and harmfulness. This is called right intention.

And what, monks, is right speech? It is the refraining from lying, from slander, from harsh speech, and from idle chatter. This is called right speech.

And what, monks, is right action? It is refraining from killing, from stealing, and from sexual misconduct. This is called right action.

And what, monks, is right livelihood? It is when a noble disciple refrains from wrongful ways of earning a living and adopts rightful ones. This is called right livelihood.

And what, monks, is right effort? It is when a monk rouses his will, makes an effort, exerts the mind, and strives to prevent from arising unskillful states of mind that have not yet arisen. It is when he...strives to abandon unskillful states of mind that have

Alt Trans: DN 22.21, pp. 348-349.

already arisen. It is when he...strives to arouse skillful states of mind that have not yet arisen. It is when he...strives to maintain skillful states of mind that have arisen, not to let them fade or be lost, but to increase them, perfect them, and help them develop. This is called right effort.

And what, monks, is right mindfulness? It is when a monk keeps his mind focused on his body as body—energetic, alert, and mindful and free from desire and aversion. He keeps his mind focused on feelings as feelings..., the mind as mind, and mind objects as mind objects—energetic, alert, and mindful and free from desire and aversion. This is called right mindfulness.

And what is right concentration? It is when a monk, detached from sensual desires and free from unskillful mental states, enters and remains in the first *jhāna*—a state of directed thoughts and judgments, filled with rapture and bliss. With the stilling of thoughts and judgments, he enters and remains in the second *jhāna*—a state of clarity, confidence, and unity, filled with rapture and bliss. And with the fading away of rapture, he enters and remains in the third *jhāna*—a state of equanimity, mindfulness, and awareness...of which the noble ones declare "with equanimity and mindfulness, he meditates in bliss." With the abandon of pleasure and pain and the disappearance of his former happiness and sadness, he enters and remains in the fourth *jhāna*—a state of pure equanimity and mindfulness, beyond pleasure and pain. This is called right concentration.

This is called the noble truth of the path leading to the cessation of suffering.

Advice to Rahula
[Ambalatthikarahulovada Sutta]

Thus have I heard.
On one occasion, the Blessed one was staying in the Squirrels' Sanctuary in the Bamboo Grove near Rajagaha. At that time the Venerable Rahula was staying at Ambalat-

---

Alt Trans: MN 61, pp. 523-526.

thika. When evening came, the Blessed One emerged from his meditation and went to Ambalatthika to see the Venerable Rahula. Seeing him approaching from the distance, the Venerable Rahula prepared a seat for him and set out some water for washing his feet. The Blessed One sat down on the seat that had been prepared for him, and, while seated, washed his feet. The Venerable Rahula greeted the Blessed One and sat down beside him.

The Analogy of the Water Vessel

When there was only a small quantity of water left in the water vessel, the Blessed One asked, "Rahula, do you see this little bit of water remaining in the water vessel?"

"Yes, Venerable One."

"That is how insignificant the contemplative practice is in anyone who has no shame in telling a deliberate lie."

Then the Blessed One threw away the small amount of water remaining in the water vessel and asked, "Rahula, do you see how this little bit of water is tossed away?"

"Yes, Venerable One."

"That is how discarded the contemplative practice is in anyone who has no shame in telling a deliberate lie."

Then the Blessed One turned the water vessel right side up again and asked, "Rahula, do you see how empty and hollow this water vessel is?"

"Yes, Venerable One."

"That is how empty and hollow the contemplative practice is of anyone who has no shame in telling a deliberate lie...."

"Rahula in this way should you train yourself: "I will not tell a deliberate lie even in jest."

The Practice of Moral Self-Reflection

"Tell me, Rahula: What is a mirror for?"

"For reflection, Venerable One."

"In the same way, Rahula, bodily action, verbal actions, and mental actions ought to be done only after repeated reflection."

Reflection Upon Bodily Actions

[Future Actions] "Whenever you want to perform some bodily action, you should reflect in this way: 'Would this bodily action that I am about to perform cause harm to myself, cause harm to others, or cause harm to both myself and others? Is it an unskillful bodily action that would lead to suffering and pain?' If upon reflection you know that, 'This bodily action I am about to perform would cause harm to myself, would cause harm to others, or would cause harm to both myself and others; it is an unskillful bodily action, leading to suffering and pain'...then you should not perform such a bodily action. But, if upon reflection, you know 'This bodily action I am about to perform would *not* cause harm to myself, would *not* cause harm to others, and would *not* cause harm to both myself and others; it is a skillful bodily action, leading to pleasure and happiness...then you may perform such a bodily action."

[Present Actions] "While you are performing some bodily action, you should reflect in this way: 'Is this bodily action that I am doing causing harm to myself, causing harm to others, or causing harm to both myself and others? Is it an unskillful bodily action leading to suffering and pain?' If upon reflection you know that, 'This bodily action I am doing is causing harm to myself, is causing harm to others, or is causing harm to both myself and others; it is an unskillful bodily action, leading to suffering and pain'... then you should not continue to perform such a bodily action. But, if upon reflection, you know 'This bodily action I am doing does *not* cause harm to myself, does *not* cause harm to others, and does *not* cause harm to both myself and others; it is a skillful bodily action, leading to pleasure and happiness...then you may continue to perform such a bodily action."

[Past Actions] "Having completed some bodily action, you should reflect in this way: 'Did this bodily action that I have just done cause harm to myself, cause harm to others, or cause harm to both myself and others? Was it an unskillful bodily action leading to suffering and pain?' If upon reflection you know that, 'This bodily action that I have just done caused harm to myself, caused harm to others, or caused harm to both myself and others; it was an unskillful bodily action, that led to suffering and pain'...

then you should confess it and lay it open to a teacher or some wise companions in the holy life. Having confessed it, you should exercise restraint in the future. But, if upon reflection, you know 'This bodily action I have just done did *not* cause harm to myself, did *not* cause harm to others, and did *not* cause harm to both myself and others; it was a skillful bodily action, that led to pleasure and happiness…then you can abide in happiness and joy, training day and night in wholesome states."

Reflection Upon Verbal Actions [Speech]

[Future Actions] "Whenever you want to perform some verbal action, you should reflect in this way: 'Would this verbal action that I am about to perform cause harm to myself, cause harm to others, or cause harm to both myself and others? Is it an unskillful bodily action that would lead to suffering and pain?' If upon reflection you know that, 'This verbal action I am about to perform would cause harm to myself, would cause harm to others, or would cause harm to both myself and others; it is an unskillful verbal action, leading to suffering and pain'…then you should not perform such a verbal action. But, if upon reflection, you know 'This verbal action I am about to perform would *not* cause harm to myself, would *not* cause harm to others, and would *not* cause harm to both myself and others; it is a skillful bodily action, leading to pleasure and happiness…then you may perform such a verbal action."

[Present Actions] "While you are performing some verbal action…[if] upon reflection you know that, 'This verbal action I am doing is causing harm…,' then you should not continue to perform such a bodily action. But, if upon reflection, you know 'This verbal action I am doing does *not* cause harm…then you may continue to perform such a bodily action."

[Past Actions] "Having completed some verbal action…[if] upon reflection you know that, 'This verbal action that I have just done caused harm…,' [then] [h]aving confessed it, you should exercise restraint in the future. But, if upon reflection, you know 'This verbal action I have just done did *not* cause harm…then you can abide in happiness and joy, training day and night in wholesome states."

Reflection Upon Mental Actions [Thoughts]

[Future Actions] "Whenever you want to perform some mental action, you should reflect in this way: 'Would this mental action that I am about to perform cause harm to myself, cause harm to others, or cause harm to both myself and others? Is it an unskillful mental action that would lead to suffering and pain?' If upon reflection you know that, 'This mental action I am about to perform would cause harm to myself, would cause harm to others, or would cause harm to both myself and others; it is an unskillful mental action, leading to suffering and pain'...then you should not perform such a mental action. But, if upon reflection, you know 'This mental action I am about to perform would *not* cause harm to myself, would *not* cause harm to others, and would *not* cause harm to both myself and others; it is a skillful bodily action, leading to pleasure and happiness...then you may perform such a mental action."

[Present Actions] "While you are performing some mental action...[if] upon reflection you know that, 'This mental action I am doing is causing harm...,' then you should not continue to perform such a mental action. But, if upon reflection, you know 'This mental action I am doing does *not* cause harm...then you may continue to perform such a mental action."

[Past Actions] "Having completed some verbal action...[if] upon reflection you know that, 'This mental action that I have just done caused harm...,' then you should feel distressed, ashamed, and disgusted with it. Feeling distressed, ashamed, and disgusted with it, you should exercise restraint in the future. But, if upon reflection, you know 'This verbal action I have just done did *not* cause harm...then you can abide in happiness and joy, training day and night in wholesome states."

Reflection and Moral Purification

"Rahula, all those brahmins and contemplatives in the past who purified their bodily, verbal, and mental actions, did it through repeated reflection on their actions in just this way."

"Rahula, all those brahmins and contemplatives in the future who will purify their bodily, verbal, and mental actions, will do it through repeated reflection on their actions in just this way."

"Rahula, all those brahmins and contemplatives in the present who will purify their bodily, verbal, and mental actions, do it through repeated reflection on their actions in just this way."

"Therefore, Rahula, you should train yourself: 'I will purify my bodily actions through repeated reflection. I will purify my verbal actions through repeated reflection. I will purify my mental actions through repeated reflection.' This is how you should train yourself."

This is what the Blessed One said, and the Venerable Rahula delighted in his words.

Cultivating Skillful States of Mind

The Divine Abodes
[Tevijja Sutta]

[A disciple] lets his mind pervade one quarter of the world with a mind imbued with *loving kindness*, then the second quarter, then the third quarter, then the fourth quarter. Thus he pervades the whole world—above, below, around, everywhere—with a mind imbued with loving-kindness, vast, deep, boundless, without hatred or ill-will.

Then he pervades one quarter with a mind imbued with *compassion*, then the second quarter, then the third quarter, then the fourth quarter. Thus he pervades the whole world—above, below, around, everywhere—with a mind imbued with compassion, vast, deep, boundless, without hatred or ill-will.

Then he pervades one quarter with a mind imbued with *sympathetic joy*, then the second quarter, then the third quarter, then the fourth quarter. Thus he pervades the whole world—above, below, around, everywhere—with a mind imbued with sympathetic joy, vast, deep, boundless, without hatred or ill-will.

Then he pervades one quarter with a mind imbued with *equanimity*, then the second quarter, then the third quarter, then the

---

Alt Trans: DN 13.76-79, pp. 194-195.

fourth quarter. Thus he pervades the whole world—above, below, around, everywhere—with a mind imbued with equanimity vast, deep, boundless, without hatred or ill-will.

Just as a mighty trumpeter makes himself heard without difficulty in all four directions, so [the disciple] does not pass by or leave aside any things in this world, but regards them all with his mind set free through deep-felt loving-kindness, [compassion, sympathetic joy, and equanimity].

This is the way to union with Brahma.

The Similie of the Saw
[Kakacupama Sutta]

Monks, even if bandits were to carve you up limb by limb with a two-handled saw, he among you who allowed his heart to get angered even then would not be obeying my teaching. Even then, you should train yourselves like this: "Our minds will be unaffected and we will speak no evil words. We will remain sympathetic for the welfare of that person, with minds filled with good will and no hatred in our hearts. We will keep pervading him with radiant thoughts of love, and beginning with him will pervade the entire world with radiant thoughts of love—vast, deep, boundless, free from hatred and ill-will." This is how you should train yourself.

Meditation on Loving-Kindness
[Metta Sutta]

One who is skillful in the ways of goodness and who seeks to attain the state of perfect tranquility should act in this way:
He should be able and perfectly upright,
gentle in speech, humble, and not arrogant,
well-content, easily satisfied,
freed from unnecessary duties, living simply,
self-controlled, prudent, and modest,

Alt Trans: Kakacupama Sutta: MN 21, p. 223; Metta Sutta: SN 1.8.

not greedily attached to mundane things.
He should refrain from committing any acts
of which the wise might disapprove.

Contemplating, in happiness and safety,
may all beings find happiness.
Whatever beings there may be—whether weak or strong,
large and mighty, medium, short, or small,
those visible and those invisible,
those dwelling far away and those nearby,
those who are born and those yet to be born...
may they all, without exception, find happiness.

Let no one work to undermine another,
or despise another in any way;
through anger or through malicious thoughts,
let no one wish harm upon another.

Just as a mother would protect her only child,
even at the risk of her own life,
so too should one cultivate a boundless mind
towards all living creatures.

Cultivate a mind of loving-kindness
boundlessly directed towards the entire world,
above and below and all around—
without reservations
and without hatred or ill-will.

Whether standing, walking, sitting
or lying down (as long as one is free from drowsiness),
one should sustain this mindfulness—
known as the divine abiding here.

By not falling into (wrongful) views,
one with virtue and endowed with perfect vision,
who is freed from all sense desire,
is not again born into this world.

Mental Development
[The Dhammapada]

I. The Twin Verses

1. Everything that we are is a result of our thoughts: by our thoughts all is founded; by our thoughts all is fashioned. If one speaks or acts with impure thoughts, suffering inevitably follows, just like the wheels of a cart follow the ox that pulls it.

2. Everything that we are is a result of our thoughts: by our thoughts all is founded; by our thoughts all is fashioned. If one speaks or acts with pure thoughts, happiness inevitably follows, like a shadow that never leaves.

3. "He abused me, he hit me, he overcame me, he robbed me." Those who harbor such thoughts will never be freed of hatred.

4. "He abused me, he hit me, he overcame me, he robbed me." Those who do not harbor such thoughts overcome their hatred.

5. For hatred can never be overcome by hatred. It can only be overcome by love. This is an eternal law....

II. Mind

33. Just as a fletcher straightens an arrow shaft, so the wise man straightens his wavering and unsteady mind, which is so difficult to master.

34. Like a fish, when pulled out of the water and stranded on dry land, our mind thrashes and quivers, desperate to escape the realm of Mara.

35. It is hard to train the mind, which goes where it wants and does what it wants. But a tamed mind brings happiness.

36. Let the wise man guard his mind, which is subtle and wily. For, a guarded mind brings happiness

37. Those who can subdue their mind, [which wanders about aimlessly,] are freed from the bonds of Mara.

38. Wisdom can never be perfected in one whose mind is un-

Alt Trans: DMP, 78, 87-88.

steady and not serene and who doesn't know the *dhamma*.

39. There is no fear for a man whose mind is awakened, freed from lust, and who has gone beyond thoughts of merit and de-merit.

40. Knowing that this body is as fragile as a clay pot, and mak-ing his mind like a fortress, one should fight Mara with the weap-on of wisdom and be ever-vigilant after this conquest.

41. Before very long this body will lie in the ground, despised and without consciousness, like a useless log.

42. Whatever harm an enemy may do to an enemy, a hater to a hater, an untrained mind will do even greater harm to you.

43. Neither a mother, father, or any other family member can do greater good for you than your own well-trained mind.

Temple Buddhas (Wat Chaiwatthanaran, Ayutthya, Thailand, 17th century)

CHAPTER VIII

Meditative Practice

In the last chapter it was noted that the last three steps of the Buddha's Noble Eightfold Path were focused on mental development and the last two, in particular, on the most well-known Buddhist meditative practices—namely right concentration and right mindfulness. More than any other spiritual tradition, Buddhism emphasizes meditation as a vital path on the role to liberation. Meditation is so closely associated with Buddhism that one could argue that there really can be no authentic Buddhism without some kind of consistent meditative practice.

Interestingly, there is no precise term for meditation in early Buddhist literature. The word that is generally used is "*bhavana*," which literally means "to cultivate," "to produce," or "to bring into being." In general the term refers to the cultivation of skillful states of mind that aid in the attainment of enlightenment.

The Buddha emphasized two different forms of meditation: *samatha* and *vipassana*. *Samatha* (tranquility) meditation aims at developing deep states of concentration (*samadhi*) in order to attain peace. Despite the confusing use of different terms, *samatha* essentially refers to the same practice as *samadhi* (concentration) in the Eightfold Path. *Vipassana* (insight) meditation aims to develop wisdom (*panna*) to end suffering through a deep insight into the nature of bodily and mental processes. In order to attain this insight some degree of concentration is required, so *samatha* is often considered to be a precondition for *vipassana*.

Samatha

The Buddha believed that our original mind is clean and pure, but it can become stained by defilements (*kilesas*). "Luminous is the mind," the Buddha told his monks, "but sometimes it is defiled by [external] defilements. The uninstructed [man] does not understand it as it really is" (AN 1.10, p. 97). To use a common analogy in Buddhism, the mind of most people is like a pond that has been stirred up. The turbulence of the water has caused so much muck to arise that we can no longer see the bottom of the pond.

What the Buddha maintained is that we need to return the mind to its original state of clarity and stillness. In keeping with the above analogy, we need to find some way to keep the pond free of disturbance so that its waters will be totally clear. The way to do this is through the technique of *samatha* meditation, which involves developing the capacity of the mind to experience full concentration (*samadhi*)—to rest undisturbed on a single object of concentration.

Of course, the most common object of concentration is the breath, but in fact we can use just about anything around us—sites, sounds, tastes, objects of touch, etc.—to focus and calm the mind. The Theravada tradition of Buddhism, in fact, emphasizes 40 objects ("*kammatthana*" or literally "places to work") suitable for *samatha* meditation. These include ten kasinas (visual objects), ten foul objects, ten recollections, four Divine Abodes, four Formless realms, one perception, and one analysis of the Four Elements. Traditionally, these objects of meditation were assigned to students by their teacher based upon the student's particular level of meditative ability and personality.

The basic practice of *samatha* meditation is actually quite straightforward: One sits in a comfortable but alert posture and places one's mind on an appropriate object of meditation. When a hindrance arises that distracts the mind, one simply returns one's attention to the object. At first, one's mind will experience countless distractions and it will be necessary time and again to return one's attention to the object of meditation. With diligence and much practice, most people eventually find that they are able to concentrate for longer and longer periods of time.

Of course, *samatha* meditation may seem quite simple in theory, but anyone who's ever tried it knows that the mind plays its own games that often interfere with developing deep states of concentration and calm. These games that the mind plays are known in Buddhist literature as "The Five Hindrances" (AN 5.23, p. 641; DN 22.13, p. 341):

1. sensual desire: cravings involving the five sense objects (touch, taste, sight, sound, smell).
2. aversion: negative thoughts concerning objects of anger, hatred, and resentment.
3. sloth and drowsiness: a dullness of mind that drags one into inertia.
4. restlessness and worry: agitation of the mind that makes it difficult to calm down.
5. doubt: lack of conviction and trust.

At one point or another, just about every meditator will be forced to contend with one or more of these hindrances, since their presence makes meditation itself difficult, if not impossible. They are a particular problem for meditation novices and can often lead such individuals to abandon meditative practice entirely out of frustration. The worst strategy for dealing with the hindrances is to get angry or frustrated about them, since this only serves to add fuel to the fire. A much better option is to use the tools of mindfulness practice, described in the next section, to try to study the hindrances objectively, noting their arising and passing away, until they lose their power to interfere with the act of concentration.

Eventually, the mind settles down and the meditator attains a state of stillness and peace that is quite different from the ordinary turbulent state of the mind. In Buddhism such a state of deep calm is known as a *jhāna* (San: *dhāyna*)—a trance-like state that leads to feelings of ecstasy or bliss. There are actually four *jhānas* described by the Buddha, which involve deeper and deeper levels of absorption (AN 5.28; MN 111). At the level of the first *jhāna*, the mind continues to engage in discursive thinking, but pleasant sensations (rapture, joy) tend to occur which make meditation much more enjoyable than it might previously have been. At the highest levels of *jhānas* an advanced meditator may even develop super-human powers.

As powerful as *jhāna* states may be to the meditator, however, the Buddha clearly did not see these states as ends in themselves. Although he believed that a certain degree of mental stability and calm is necessary for the practice of meditation, the Buddha viewed these states as temporary and thought that something more was needed in order to end suffering. This "something more"—the truly original innovation of the Buddha with respect to meditative practice—is *vipassana*, or insight meditation, as it is more commonly known.

Vipassana

The word *vipassana* is derived from two words: "*vi,*" which means "in various ways," and "*passana,*" which means "to see." *Vipassana*, therefore, literally means "to see in various ways." *Vipassana* or mindfulness meditation aims at achieving by direct experience the deep understanding of one's own nature and the nature of all things as characterized by impermanence, no-self, and suffering. Using the example of the pond again, it is believed in Buddhism that once disturbances in the pond (the mind) have been stilled (through the practice of *samatha* meditation), then one can begin to see the bottom of the pond (to penetrate into the very nature of reality though *vipassana* meditation).

The main source that we have for the Buddha's teachings on mindfulness meditation is from the *Satipatthana Sutta* (*Discourse on the Four Foundations of Mindfulness*). The word "*satipatthana*" is derived from two Pali words: "*sati,*" which means awareness of what is happening in the present moment with regards to the body and mind and "*patthana,*" which means "to set firmly." As Bhikkhu Bodhi points out, however, the awareness achieved through the practice of mindfulness differs from other kinds of awareness in our everyday lives:

All consciousness involves awareness in the sense of a knowing or experiencing of an object. But with the practice of mindfulness awareness is applied at a special pitch. The mind is deliberately kept at the level of *bare attention*, a detached observation of what is happening within us and around us at the present moment.

In the practice of...mindfulness, the mind is trained to remain in the present, open, quiet, and alert, contemplating the present event. All judgments and interpretations have to be suspended, or if they occur, just registered and dropped. The task is simply to note whatever comes up just as it is occurring, riding the changes of events in the way a surfer rides the waves on the sea. The whole process is a way of coming back to the present, of standing in the here and now without slipping away, without getting swept away by the tides of distracting thoughts (76).

The problem for most of us is that we rarely dwell attentively in the present moment. Almost as soon as we experience anything in life (the birth of a child, for example), our minds immediately begins to spin reactive thoughts about this event ("I wonder if I'll be a good mother" or "What if the baby gets sick after I bring him home?") What mindfulness practice teaches us is the vital skill of just being present with an experience—whatever it may be—and allowing it to be just as it is, rather than how we would like it to be.

The practice that the Buddha describes in the sutta is at the same time both amazingly simple, yet maddeningly complex for most people: it involves direct awareness of experience without falling into the trap of forming judgments or engaging in conceptual elaborations about that experience. The goal, therefore, is to "bring to light experience in its pure immediacy"—that is, before it gets colored by our own conceptual elaborations (Bodhi, 77). That may seem simple enough until you actually attempt it. Try mindfully observing an emotion, for example, as it arises within you and see how long you can maintain bare awareness without allowing reactive thoughts, fantasies, or judgments to color over this experience. If you're like most people, conceptualizations begin to occur almost instantaneously...and then you've lost the essence of the experience in itself. You're reacting to the experience, rather than simply being present with it.

Although mindfulness can be applied to just about any experience, in the *Satipatthana Sutta* the Buddha describes four specific areas for the cultivation of mindfulness: mindfulness of the body, of the feelings, of the mind, and of mind-states. These have become known as the "four foundations" of mindfulness.

Mindfulness of the Body (Kaya)

In contemplating the body, the Buddha tells us to focus on the "body in itself." In other words, we are to look at the body as it actually is rather than how we would like it to be. As part of this practice, the Buddha offers 14 possible subjects for contemplation: (1) Mindfulness of the breath (*anapanasati*), (2) The four postures; standing, walking, sitting, and lying down, (3) Daily activities; (4) Repulsiveness of the 32 parts of the body; (5) The four material elements; (6) Nine cemetery contemplations.

The most common practice in *vipassana* is to use the breath as a means to develop mindfulness. In *samatha* meditation it was enough simply to focus on the sensation of the breath as it passes in and out of your nose. In *vipassana*, the meditator is now instructed to place his attention on the specific quality of the breath: is it short or long, shallow or deep, etc. The goal is not to think about the breath or form judgments about it, but simply to observe it mindfully.

This same practice is then applied to mindful awareness of one's specific posture (walking, standing, sitting, lying down) and the change from one posture to another. We also apply the same sort of attentiveness to the various bodily activities that we engage in during the course of the day (eating, drinking, defecating, talking, etc.). It's important to note that mindfulness meditation doesn't just occur while sitting on a cushion or engaged in formal meditation. The Buddha expected us to be mindful all day long and in everything that we do.

The practice of mindfulness of the breath in particular can be considered foundational because it necessarily roots one in the present: as long as you're focused on the breath as it is, for example, you can't be in the past, the future, or in some fantasy realm. The skill developed through this practice makes it easier when you then turn to more subtle, internal phenomena like feelings and thoughts.

Mindfulness of Sensation (Vedana)

As one sits mindfully attuned to the body, one begins to notice that physical sensations or sense impressions arise all the time throughout the body. There's the itch on your arm, the pressure on your ankles as you sit cross-legged, perhaps the grumbling of your stomach as it reminds you that you haven't eaten in a while. In experiencing sensations, one also tends to experience them as pleasant, unpleasant, or neutral (neither pleasant nor unpleasant). It is these particular qualities of sensations that the Buddha is referring to when he talks about the contemplating "*vedana.*"

Unfortunately, no English translation of the term is totally adequate. More often than not *vedana* is translated as "feeling," which might lead readers to conclude that what the Buddha is talking about is something like "emotions." But *vedana* are clearly not emotions, which are more complex phenomena and specifically addressed in the next foundation of mindfulness. I've opted to translate *vedana* as "sensation" because in several suttas the Buddha specifically describes the origins of *vedana* as arising from connection with the body and senses (SN 36.7, 8, pp. 1266-1269; AN 6.63, 960). It should be kept in mind, however, that the Buddha believed that *vedana* could also involve internal (i.e., spiritual, unworldly) sensations, like the rapture or bliss arising from a *jhāna* state.

Why are sensations so important as objects of mindful contemplation? The answer is that the way we react to sensations can often lead us to engage in unskillful behavior. Pleasant sensations can trigger greed or craving; unpleasant sensations can trigger hatred or aversion. But this process only happens when we are not mindful of these sensations and their particular qualities. Then we are likely to react impulsively—at times causing greater suffering for ourselves and others.

Instead, what mindfulness teaches us is simply to observe all sensations with equanimity, neither indulging them nor rejecting them. Eventually, if we can learn to just sit with the various sensations that we experience, we notice that these sensations arise and eventually pass away. When we begin to see that sensations are impermanent, they can be seen for what they are—an endless stream of sensory experiences. And it is with this insight that our normal reactive way of dealing with sensations begins to be transformed into something much more skillful.

Mindfulness of Mind-States (Citta)

The term "*citta*" in Buddhist literature is usually translated "mind." The problem with this translation is that in the West we tend to think of the mind solely in terms of thoughts, while in Buddhism what is called "mind" involves both thoughts and emotions. Thus among the various types of *citta* that the Buddha notes, are the mind with lust, the mind with aversion, the mind with delusion, the collected mind, the scattered mind, the expansive mind, the unexpansive mind, the surpassed mind, the unsurpassed mind, the concentrated mind, the unconcentrated mind, the liberated mind, the unliberated mind. A much better translation of "*citta*", therefore, would be "mind-states," which carries a more emotive connotation.

Like sensations, these *citta* flicker through the mind, coming and going in rapid succession. Through the process of mindfully observing these mind-states, we begin to notice that they too are impermanent. We also begin to become aware that these *citta* are not self—that they don't belong to "me."

Mindfulness of Mind-Objects (Dhammas)

The most difficult of the four foundations of mindfulness for many people to get a handle on is what is known as Mindfulness of *dhammas*. The problem here is that the term "*dhamma*" can refer to the teachings of the Buddha or can refer to things, phenomena, or aspects of reality. These phenomena however, are only significant insofar as they are objects of the mind. "Mind objects," in this case, seems to be the optimal translation for "*dhammas*." The phenomena specifically investigated in this section of the sutta are the five hindrances, the five aggregates, the six inner and outer sense bases, the seven factors of enlightenment and the Four Noble Truths.

In the *Satipatthana Sutta*, the practice of mindfulness is described as the most direct or the straightest way "for the overcoming of sorrow and misery for the destruction of pain and grief." Some have actually translated this passage as "the only path" or the "unifying path" for the realization of *Nibbāna* (see Anālayo, 27). However it's translated, it's clear that the Buddha placed a premium on the practice of mindfulness meditation as one of the most effective and efficient means to attain *Nibbāna*.

The reason for this should be evident by now: mindfulness practice enables one to penetrate into the very essence of reality, providing a "direct experience" of—rather than conceptual knowledge about—the three qualities of all things that we discussed earlier in this text: impermanence, non-self, and suffering. Observing things like sensations, mind-states, and mind-objects, we see for ourselves how these things arise and how they pass away, how they are not "me," and how attachment leads to suffering and non-attachment to freedom from suffering.

READING THE SOURCES

~~~

Samatha and Vipassana
[Vijja-Bhagiya Sutta]

Two things, monks, are required for true knowledge. What are these two? Tranquility (*samatha*) and insight (*vipassana*). What benefit does one experience from the development of tranquility? The mind is developed. And what benefit does one experience when the mind is developed? Passion is abandoned. What benefit does one experience from the development of insight? Wisdom is developed. And what benefit does one experience when wisdom is developed? Ignorance is abandoned.

The Five Hindrances
[Mahasatipatthana Sutta]

How does a monk meditate...with respect to the five hindrances?

Here a monk who has *sensual desire* present in him clearly knows that he has sensual desire in him. If sensual desire is not present in him, he clearly knows that sensual desire is not present in him. And he clearly knows how sensual desire that has not yet arisen comes to arise; how sensual desire that has arisen comes to be abandoned; and how sensual desire that has been abandoned comes not to rise again in the future.

If *aversion* is present in him, he knows that it is present. If aversion is not present in him, he clearly knows that aversion is

---

Alt. Trans: Samatha and Vipassana: AN 2.30, p. 152, ; The Five Hindrances: DN 22.13, p. 341.

not present in him. And he clearly knows how aversion that has not yet arisen comes to arise; how aversion that has arisen comes to be abandoned; and how aversion that has been abandoned comes not to rise again in the future.

If *dullness and drowsiness* are present in him, he clearly knows that dullness and drowsiness are present in him. If dullness and drowsiness are not present in him, he clearly knows that dullness and drowsiness are not present in him. And he clearly knows how dullness and drowsiness that have not yet arisen come to arise; how dullness and drowsiness that have arisen come to be abandoned; and how dullness and drowsiness that have been abandoned come not to rise again in the future.

If *restlessness and worry* are present in him, he clearly knows that restlessness and worry are present in him. If restlessness and worry are not present in him, he clearly knows that restlessness and worry are not present in him. And he clearly knows how restlessness and worry that have not yet arisen come to arise; how restlessness and worry that have arisen come to be abandoned; and how restlessness and worry that have been abandoned come not to rise again in the future.

If *doubt* is present in him, he clearly knows that doubt is present in him. If doubt is not present in him, he clearly knows that doubt is not present in him. And he clearly knows how doubt that has not yet arisen comes to arise; how doubt that has arisen comes to be abandoned; and how doubt that has been abandoned comes not to rise again in the future.

The Foundations of Mindfulness
[Satipatthana Sutta]

Thus have I heard.
At one time the Blessed One was residing in the town of Kammasadhamma in the land of the Kurus. There the Blessed One addressed the Monks...

"Monks, this is the direct path for the purification of beings,

Alt. Trans: MN 10, pp. 145-155.

for the overcoming of sorrow and distress, for the eradication of sorrow and distress, for the attainment of the true way, for the realization of *Nibbāna*—namely, the four foundations of mindfulness.

What are these four?

Here, a monk meditates by observing the *body* (*kaya*) in itself, ardent, fully aware, and mindful, free from desire and aversion for the world.

He meditates by observing *sensations* (*vedana*) in themselves, ardent, fully aware, and mindful, free from desire and aversion for the world.

He meditates by observing the *mind-states* (*citta*) in themselves, ardent, fully aware, and mindful, free from desire and aversion for the world.

He meditates by observing *mind-objects* (*dhammas*) in themselves, fully aware, and mindful, free from desire and aversion for the world.

1. Mindfulness of the Body

Meditation on Breathing

And how does a monk meditate by observing the body in itself?

Here a monk, having gone into the wilderness, to the foot of a tree or to an empty building, sits down with his legs crossed and his body erect, and directs his mindfulness to the object of mindfulness—namely, the breath that is in front of him. Mindfully, he breathes in; mindfully, he breathes out.

Breathing in deeply, he knows, 'I am breathing in deeply.' Breathing out deeply, he knows, 'I am breathing out deeply.'

Breathing in shallowly, he knows, 'I am breathing in shallowly.' Breathing out shallowly, he knows, 'I am breathing out shallowly.'

He practices in this way: 'Breathing in, I experience the whole body breath....Breathing out, I experience the whole body breath.'

He practices in this way: 'Breathing in, I calm the energy of the [in-breath]....Breathing out, I calm the energy of the [out-breath].'....

Thus, he meditates by focusing on the body in itself internally, the body as body externally, or he focuses on the body in itself both internally and externally. He meditates by focusing on things as they arise in the body or things as they pass away in the body, or things as they arise and pass away in the body.

Or he meditates mindful that 'There is a body' to the extent necessary for bare knowledge and awareness. He meditates independently, not clinging to the things of the world. This too is how a monk meditates by observing the body in itself.

Meditation on Bodily Postures

Furthermore, when walking, the monk knows, 'I am walking.' When standing, he knows 'I am standing.' When sitting, he knows 'I am sitting.' When lying down, he knows, 'I am lying down.' Or whatever posture his body is in, he knows this....

Meditation on Bodily Activity

When going forward or backwards...,when looking ahead or behind..., when bending or stretching his limbs..., when wearing his robes or carrying his alms bowls..., when eating, drinking, chewing, or tasting, when defecating and urinating..., when walking, standing, sitting, falling asleep, waking up, talking, and remaining silent...he is aware of this.

Thus, he meditates by focusing on the body in itself internally, the body in itself externally, or he focuses on the body in itself both internally and externally. He meditates independently, not clinging to the things of the world. This too is how a monk meditates by observing the body in itself....

2. Mindfulness of Sensation

And how does a monk meditate by observing sensations in themselves?

Here, when experiencing a pleasant sensation he knows, 'I am experiencing a pleasant sensation.'

When experiencing an unpleasant sensation, he knows, 'I am experiencing an unpleasant sensation.'

Or, when experiencing a sensation that is neither pleasant nor unpleasant, he knows, 'I am experiencing a sensation that is neither pleasant nor unpleasant.'

When experiencing a pleasant (unpleasant, neither pleasant nor unpleasant) physical sensation, he knows, 'I am experiencing a pleasant (unpleasant, neither pleasant nor unpleasant) physical sensation.'

When experiencing a pleasant (unpleasant, neither pleasant nor unpleasant) non-physical sensation, he knows, 'I am experiencing a pleasant (unpleasant, neither pleasant nor unpleasant) non-physical sensation.'

Thus he meditates by focusing on sensations in themselves internally, sensations in themselves externally, or sensations in themselves both internally and externally. Or he meditates on sensations as they arise, or on feelings as they pass away, or on feelings as they arise and pass away.

Or he meditates mindful that 'This is a sensation' to the extent necessary for bare knowledge and awareness. He meditates independently, not clinging to the things of the world. This too is how a monk meditates by observing feelings in themselves.

3. Mindfulness of Mind-States

And how does a monk meditate by observing the mind-states in themselves

Here, a monk knows a mind with desire as 'a mind with desire' and a mind without desire as 'a mind without desire.'

He knows a mind with aversion as 'a mind with aversion' and a mind without aversion as 'a mind without aversion.'

He knows a mind with delusion as 'a mind with delusion' and a mind without delusion as 'a mind without delusion.'

He knows a mind that is collected as 'a mind that is collected' and he knows a mind that is scattered as 'a mind that is scattered.'

He knows a mind that is expansive as 'a mind that is expansive' and he knows a mind that is not expansive as 'a mind that is not expansive.'

He knows a mind that is surpassed as 'a mind that is surpassed' and he knows a mind that is not surpassed as 'a mind that is not surpassed.'

He knows a mind that is concentrated as 'a mind that is concentrated' and he knows a mind that is not concentrated as 'a mind that is not concentrated.'

He knows a mind that is liberated as 'a mind that is liberated' and he knows a mind that is not liberated as 'a mind that is not liberated.'

Thus he meditates by focusing on the mind-state in itself internally, the mind-state in itself externally, or the mind-state in itself both internally and externally. Or he meditates on mind-states as they arise, or on mind-states as they pass away, or on mind-states as they arise and pass away.

Or he meditates mindful that 'This is a mind-state' to the extent necessary for bare knowledge and awareness. He meditates independently, not clinging to the things of the world. This too is how a monk meditates by observing the mind-states in themselves.

4. Mindfulness of Mind-Objects

And how does a monk meditate by observing mind-objects in themselves?

Here a monk meditates by observing mind-objects with respect to the *five hindrances*....He knows when sensual desire... anger...sloth and lethargy...restlessness and worry...doubt is present within him. He knows when [these things are] not within him. He knows how [these things come] to arise. He knows how [these things come] to be abandoned. He knows how once abandoned [these things come] not to arise again in the future....

Here a monk meditates by observing mind-objects with respect to the *five aggregates*....He knows what material form... feeling...perception...volition...consciousness is.   He knows how [these things come] to arise. He knows how [these things come] to pass away.

Here a monk meditates by observing mind-objects with respect to the *six internal and external sense fields*....He knows the eye and objects of sight...the ear and sounds...the nose and smells... the tongue and taste...the body and objects of touch...the mind and objects of thought....He knows how attachments arise with respect to [these things]. He knows how an attachment that has not yet arisen with respect to [these things come] to arise. He knows how attachments once arisen with respect to [these things], can be abandoned. He knows how abandoned attachments with respect to [these things come] not to arise again in the future....

Here a monk meditates by observing mind-objects with respect to the *seven factors of awakening*...He knows when mindfulness...investigation...energy...joy...tranquility...concentration... equanimity is present within him. He knows when [these things are] not present within him. He knows how [these things come] to arise. He knows how [these things come] to be abandoned. He knows how once abandoned [these things come] not to arise again in the future....

Here a monk meditates by observing mind-objects with respect to the *four noble truths*....He knows what suffering is... what the cause of suffering is...what the cessation of suffering is...what the path leading to the cessation of suffering is....

Thus he meditates by focusing on mind-objects in themselves internally, mind-states in themselves externally, or mind-states in themselves both internally and externally. Or he meditates on mind-states as they arise, or on mind-states as they pass away, or on mind-states as they arise and pass away.

Or he meditates mindful that 'This is a mind-object' to the extent necessary for bare knowledge and awareness. He meditates independently, not clinging to the things of the world. This too is how a monk meditates by observing mind-objects in themselves.

Conclusion

Monks, anyone who develops these four foundations of mindfulness in this way for seven years can expect one of two results: either final (liberation) here and now or, if there is any remnant of grasping yet present, the state of non-returning.

Monks...anyone who develops these four foundations of mindfulness in this way for six years...for five years...for four years...for three years...for two years...for one year can expect one of two results: either final (liberation) here and now or, if there is any remnant of grasping yet present, the state of non-returning.

Monks...anyone who develops these four foundations of mindfulness in this way for seven months...for six months...

for five months...for four months...for three months...for two months...for one month...for half-a month can expect one of two results: either final (liberation) here and now or, if there is any remnant of grasping yet present, the state of non-returning.

Monks, it was for this reason that it was said, 'This is the direct path for the purification of beings, for the overcoming of sorrow and distress, for the eradication of sorrow and distress, for the attainment of the true way, for the realization of *Nibbāna*—namely, the four foundations of mindfulness.'"

This is what the Blessed One said. Delighted, the monks rejoiced in the Blessed One's words.

Reclining Gal Vihara Buddha (Polonnaruwa, Sri Lanka, 12th century)

CHAPTER IX

Kamma, Rebirth, and Nibbāna

Directly related to the discussion of the Four Noble Truths and the Eightfold Path are three topics discussed by the Buddha that are essential to his thought, but also the cause of much confusion—*kamma*, rebirth, and *Nibbāna*. The difficulty is that we can't talk about any of these concepts without potentially slipping into the dangerous area of metaphysical speculation—something that the Buddha advises us to avoid at all costs. It's also true that many Buddhists themselves perpetuate fallacious ideas about each of these concepts that owe more to Hindu doctrine than to the insights of the Buddha himself, and which have led to a great deal of confusion.

In a nutshell, however, the Buddha gave us a very clear formula that should guide us as we talk about *kamma*, rebirth, and *Nibbāna* that can be expressed in the following way:

> Whatever intentional actions one performs, good or bad, have necessary effects ("fruits") both in the present as well as in the future.

If this formulation doesn't seem all that profound, it's because it basically isn't. It's the same insight your mother probably gave you when you did something naughty and experienced the negative effects of your actions: "you get what you deserve." The Buddha did believe that we all get what we deserve in life, but, as we'll see, there's no magic or mystery involved in his understanding of what this means.

Kamma

Let's get one mistaken notion out of the way immediately: *Kamma*, as the Buddha explained it, should not be understood as an *external* system of reward or of punishment for one's actions. For example, imagine a really nasty businessman who consistently cheats his customers and who abuses and underpays his employees. According to the "law of karma," as it's popularly understood, we would expect this fellow to experience some kind of punishment for his bad behavior—if not in this life, at least in some future state. This is most certainly not, however, what the Buddha meant at all by *kamma*.

The term *kamma*—as well as its Sanskrit counterpart, *karma*—simply means "action." But what the Buddha specifically had in mind when he used the word *kamma* are actions that are the result of willful intention. "It is [intention] (*cetanā*)...," he says, "that I call *kamma*; for having willed, one acts by body, speech, or mind" (AN 3.63, p. 963). Intentional actions are actions which have future consequences—literally *"kamma phala"* or the "fruits of action." The metaphor that the Buddha uses when discussing *kamma* is derived from agriculture. Just as one plants a seed and inevitably some kind of plant springs up, so too do our actions have fruits or effects which impact others as well as ourselves. In a nutshell, good actions—actions done out of generosity, compassionate love and wisdom—bring about positive consequences to ourselves and others; bad actions—actions done out of greed, aversion, or delusion—bring about negative consequences to ourselves and others.

It's pretty obvious intentional bad actions—lying, stealing, spreading false rumors, etc.—cause harm to others. But how do they cause harm to ourselves? The answer is that repeatedly performing harmful acts shapes our character in negative ways. These deep-rooted character traits are known in Buddhism as *sankhāras* (San: *samskāras*) or "mental formations" and are formed when intentional choices are given effect in action:

The process may be likened to the work of a potter who moulds the clay into a finished shape: the soft clay is one's character, and when we have made moral choices we hold ourselves in our hands and shape our natures for good or ill. It is not hard to see how even within the course of a single lifetime particular patterns of behavior lead inexorably to certain results....The remote effects of karmic choices are referred to as the 'maturation' (*vipāka*) or 'fruit' (*phala*) of the karmic act. The metaphor is an agricultural one: performing good and bad deeds is like planting seeds that will fruit at a later date." (Keown, 40)

The bad "fruits" or effects of our bad *kamma* are twofold, affecting us in the present as well as in the future.

In the present, the bad character that we develop by intentionally performing unskillful actions weighs us down in this life. If we have a conscience, we suffer from guilt as a result of our actions. But even with no conscience at all, a person with a badly formed character has a life fraught with disorder, tension, and anxiety compared to the person who has developed a good character and acts accordingly. In short, the life of a person of bad moral character is filled with greater suffering and dissatisfaction than the life of one who consistently tries to live more skillfully.

But the Buddha also believed that there were future effects to our actions as well. And to understand what he means by this, we need to discuss another difficult concept in Buddhism—rebirth.

Rebirth

Unfortunately, there's no specific term used in the Pali Canon that is equivalent to the term "rebirth." The closest we get in the suttas is "becoming again" (Pal: *punabbhava*; San: *punarbhava*), which generally refers to the process of change from one state to another. The vagueness of the term has led some people to mistakenly believe that the Buddhist concept of rebirth is the same as the doctrine of reincarnation (also known as "transmigration") that is found in Hinduism. This is certainly not the case.

Like rebirth, the Hindu concept of reincarnation is founded upon the idea that the fruits of our actions affect our future lives.

But that's where the similarity ends. The doctrine of reincarnation is grounded in the idea that there is an enduring soul of Self (*Atman*) that continues to exist after the death of the body in some other form. This most certainly can't be a doctrine that any Buddhist could accept since, as we know, the Buddha flatly reject the idea of an enduring Self.

So how on earth are we to understand the Buddhist idea of rebirth if we also take seriously the key Buddhist concepts of impermanence and no-self. Steve Hagen, for one, interprets the concept of rebirth without any reference at all to any future state after death. For Hagen, when the Buddha spoke about rebirth he was talking specifically about moment-by-moment rebirth within this very life:

> The Buddha said that to see with right *wisdom* is to *see* that nothing holds still but exhibits only thoroughgoing flux, flow, and change. When we *see* this clearly, we no longer take seriously any notion of persistence. In other words, when we look honestly at actual experience, without adding or assuming anything extra, the notion of an abiding self does not occur.....
>
> The fact is, *within this one life span*, as we live from moment to moment, we are never a particular, unchanging person. You are not the same person you were ten or twenty years ago. In fact, you're not the same person you were ten or twenty minutes ago (44-45).

The problem with this interpretation is that the Buddha talks about *kamma*, rebirth, and *Nibbāna* in terms of future states after death throughout the suttas. So how should we interpret such statements? We have to accept on one hand that there is "something" that passes from one life to the next as the fruits of our actions—something, in fact, that is reborn—but at the same time recognize that "something" can't be anything like a personality or soul. There can't be any "you" that is reborn, in other words, because this "you" would imply an enduring Self. So what is it then that is reborn?

The answer, some argue, can be found in the common Buddhist analogy of the candle. In this analogy, one candle lights another candle, its flame seeming to pass from candle to candle. But an individual flame does not actually move from candle to candle, each of which has its own unique flame. There is no real continuation, then, of the flame—i.e., personal identity—from one candle to the next. So, if the analogy of the candle holds, what is reborn after death is not any kind of continuation of personal identity, but something more like the karmic energy that is transmitted from one life to the next.

The bottom line when it comes to dealing with rebirth is that the Buddha was incredibly vague—perhaps intentionally so—when it came to explaining this concept. We know that he believed that asking questions like, "what's going to happen to me after death?" or "will my personal actions in this life affect what happens to me in the next life?" are basically unedifying and unhelpful. The only thing we need concern ourselves about, says the Buddha time and again, is ending our suffering here and now. In this sense Hagen is right when he says that we are better off focusing on the moment-by-moment rebirth that all of us experience in this life and leave aside dubious metaphysical speculation about future lives.

Nibbāna

When it comes to the concept of *Nibbāna*, we have even more difficulties interpreting Buddha's thought than we do with the concept of rebirth, for the simple reason that the Buddha did not describe the state of *Nibbāna* in any detail. The Pali "*Nibbāna*" term is related to the Sanskrit "*Nirvana*," which was used in Hindu thought prior to the Buddha, and literally means to blow (*va*) out (*nir*). When the Buddha talks about *Nibbāna* at all it is usually in purely negative terms—as "cessation" and "extinguishing."

The closest that the Buddha comes to an actual definition of *Nibbāna* is in discussing the Third Noble Truth, where he describes *Nibbāna* as "remainderless fading away and cessation of that same craving, the giving up and relinquishing of it, freedom from it, [detachment from] it" (SN 56.11, p. 1844). Since craving is the cause of suffering, the freedom from craving is the freedom from suffering—*Nibbāna*. To put it simply, then, *Nibbāna* is a state of freedom in which one is no longer consumed by compulsive longings, desires, and attachments.

It should be noted that when he speaks about detachment from craving, the Buddha is most certainly not talking about some kind of cold, impersonal Stoic sort of detachment that aims at indifference but a more skillful way of dealing with the world and others. As you may recall from our discussion on right effort, a truly enlightened person relates to other human beings not simply by repressing unskillful states of mind, but also by cultivating the positive emotional states of compassion, loving kindness, sympathetic joy, and equanimity (The Four Divine Abodes). Far from turning a person into a cold robot, one who has freed him- or herself from craving would be a full flesh-and-blood human being with a rich emotional life and a passionate concern for other beings.

The Buddha actually talked about two different types of *Nibbāna*, both of which were possible for enlightened individuals: *Nibbāna* without remainder and *Nibbāna* with remainder. *Nibbāna* with remainder refers to the kind of *Nibbāna* that one is capable of experiencing here and now—*Nibbāna* with the five aggregates remaining. This is the kind of *Nibbāna* that the Buddha achieved on the night of his awakening and which he continued to experience during the remaining 45 years of his life. A person who attains *Nibbāna* with remainder continues to exist in the world, but without being subject to craving. *Nibbana* without remainder or final *Nibbāna* (Pal: *parinibbana*; San: *parinirvana*) is the total extinction or unbinding of all remaining physical and mental phenomenon (the five aggregates)—a state in which one is no longer subject to rebirth in any form.

What happens to an individual who attains *Nibbāna* after death is ultimately a question that the Buddha either would not or could not answer. All he was willing to say is that it is a state in which the five aggregates vanish, but it is not a state of total nothingness either. It's something, in other words, between existence and non-existence, but ultimately indescribable, because it is beyond our categories of understanding.

READING THE SOURCES

———✧———

Good and Bad Kamma
[Nidana Sutta]

Monks, there are three causes for the origination of *kamma* (actions). And what are the three? Greed is a cause for the origination of *kamma*; hatred is a cause for the origination of *kamma*; delusion is a cause for the origination of *kamma*.

When an individual's actions, monks, are performed through greed, arise from greed, are occasioned by greed, originate in greed, these actions ripen when the individual is reborn. And wherever they ripen, there he experiences the result of those actions, whether it is in the present life or in some subsequent one.

When an individual's actions, monks, are performed through hatred...these actions ripen when the individual is reborn. And wherever they ripen, there he experiences the result of those actions, whether it is in the present life or in some subsequent one.

When an individual's actions, monks, are performed through delusion...these actions ripen when the individual is reborn. And wherever they ripen, there he experiences the result of those actions, whether it is in the present life or in some subsequent one.

It is like seeds, monks, that are uninjured, unspoiled, unharmed by wind or heat, and are sound, and advantageously sown in a fertile field on well-prepared soil. If then rain falls in its proper season, then, monks, the seed grows, increases, and matures. In exactly the same way, monks, when an individual's actions are performed through greed, arise from greed, are occasioned by

———————————

Alt. Trans: AN 3.33, pp. 343-344.

greed, originate in greed, these actions ripen when the individual is reborn. And wherever they ripen, there he experiences the results of those actions, whether in the present life or in some subsequent one.

[Likewise], when an individual's actions are performed through hatred...[or]...delusion, these actions ripen when the individual is reborn. And wherever they ripen, there he experiences the results of those actions, whether in the present life or in some subsequent one.

Monks, there are three [other] causes for the origination of *kamma*. And what are the three? Non-greed is a cause for the origination of *kamma*; non-hatred is a cause for the origination of *kamma*; non-delusion is a cause for the origination of *kamma*.

Monks, when an individual's actions are performed without greed, arise without greed, are occasioned without greed, originate without greed, then any *kamma* is abandoned when greed is abandoned. It is uprooted, pulled out of the ground like the stump of a palmyra tree. It becomes non-existent and not able to spring up again in the future.

[Likewise] when a man's actions are performed without hatred...[or]...without delusion, then any *kamma* is abandoned when hatred [or delusion are] abandoned. It is uprooted, pulled out of the ground like the stump of a palmyra tree. It becomes non-existent and not able to spring up again in the future.

It is like seeds, monks, that are uninjured, unspoiled, unharmed by wind or heat, and are sound. If someone then burns them in a fire and reduces them to ashes, and, having reduced them to ashes, scatters them to the winds, or throws them into a swift-flowing river, then, monks, will those seeds be abandoned, uprooted, pulled out of the ground like the stump of a palmyra tree, and become non-existent and not able to spring up again in the future....

These, monks, are the three conditions under which actions are produced.

Whatever actions are performed
By an ignorant person
Born of greed, hatred or delusion
Whether many or few
Are experienced right here and now,

Without any other ground for it.

Therefore does a monk abandon
Greed, hatred and delusion,
And gives rise to clear knowledge,
Abandoning all bad destinations.

Rebirth is not
Transmigration
[Milindapanha]

And the king said, "Venerable Nagasena, does rebirth take place without anything transmigrating [passing over]?"
"Yes, your majesty. Rebirth takes place without anything transmigrating."

"How, Venerable Nagasena, does rebirth take place without anything transmigrating? Give an illustration."

"Your majesty, suppose a man was to light a candle from another candle. Would the light from one candle have passed over [transmigrated] to the other candle?"

"Assuredly not, Venerable One."

"In exactly the same way, your majesty, does rebirth take place without anything transmigrating."

"Give another illustration."

"Your majesty, do you remember having learnt, when you were a boy, some verse or other from your professor of poetry?"

"Yes, Venerable One."

"Your majesty, did the verse pass over [transmigrate] to you from your teacher?"

"Assuredly not, Venerable One."

"In exactly the same way, your majesty, does rebirth take place without anything transmigrating."

"You are an able man, Venerable Nagasena."

Henry Clarke Warren, trans. *Buddhism in Translation*. *Milindapanha* 71.16. Cambridge: Harvard University Press, 1896. Translation updated.

The Realization of Nibbāna
[Mahavacchagotta Sutta]

T hus have I heard.
   On one occasion the Blessed One was residing in the
squirrel's sanctuary in the bamboo grove at Rajagaha.
The wandering ascetic Vacchagotta approached the Blessed One,
exchanged greetings with him, and sat down beside him. Then
he asked…, "Tell me, Master Gotama, the Tathagata (the monk
whose mind has been liberated)—where is he reborn after death?"

"'Reborn' does not apply, Vaccha."

"Then he is not reborn."

"'Not reborn,' does not apply."

"Then he is both reborn and not reborn."

"'Reborn and not reborn' does not apply."

"Then he is neither reborn nor not reborn."

"'Neither reborn nor not reborn' does not apply to him."

"How is it when Master Gotama is asked if the monk is reborn…, not reborn…, both reborn and not reborn…, neither reborn nor not reborn, he replies that each of these 'does not apply'?
I am confused and bewildered and the measure of confidence
that I have gained through our previous conversations has disappeared."

"You ought to be confused and bewildered, Vaccha. For this
doctrine is profound, hard to see and comprehend…and is only to
be understood by the wise. For those who hold other views, hold
to other teachings and disciplines…, it is difficult to grasp. Since
this is the case, I will put some questions to you to answer as
you see fit. Tell me, Vaccha, if a fire was burning in front of you,
would you know it was burning?"

"Yes, I would, Master Gotama."

"Suppose someone were to ask you, 'This fire that is burning
in front of you—what is it dependent upon to burn?' How would
you reply?"

Sacred Books of the Buddhists. Vol. 5: *Dialogues of the Buddha*. Trans. Lord
Chalmers. London: Oxford University Press, 1926. Translation updated. Alt
Trans: MN 72, pp. 591-594.

"Being asked this question, Master Gotama, I would reply, "This fire is dependent upon grass and wood to burn.""

"And, if the fire burning in front of you had been extinguished, would you know, "This fire burning in front of me has been extinguished'?"

"Yes, I would, Master Gotama."

"And if someone asked you, 'In what direction has the extinguished fire gone—East, West, North or South?' how would you reply?"

"That does not apply, Master Gotama. The burning fire depends upon grass and wood for sustenance. Once it consumes its fuel supply, and being without fresh supplies of fuel, it is simply said to have been extinguished."

"Just in this way, Vaccha, the *Tathagata* has abandoned any material form by which one might describe him. He has cut it off at the root...and has done away with it, so that it is no longer destined for future arising. Freed from classifications in terms of material form, Vaccha, he is profound, measureless, unfathomable, like the mighty ocean. 'He is born' does not apply; 'he is not reborn' does not apply; 'he is reborn and not reborn' does not apply; 'he is neither reborn nor not reborn' does not apply. Everything by which the *Tathagata* might be denoted has passed away from him, utterly and forever....Freed from the classifications of consciousness, Vaccha, the *Tathagata* is profound, measureless, unfathomable, like the mighty ocean...."

Nibbāna
[Udana]

Thus have I heard.

On a certain occasion the Blessed One was staying near Savvatthi at Jeta's Grove at Anathapindika's Monastery. At that time the Blessed One was instructing...the monks with a discourse on the subject of Nibbana. And these monks receptively and attentively focused their entire attentions onto this teaching.

Alt Trans: UD 8.1, 8.3, pp. 96-97.

Recognizing the significance, the Blessed One on that occasion spoke these words:

"There is, monks, a dimension, where there is neither earth, nor water, nor fire, nor wind, neither infinity of space, nor infinity of consciousness, nor nothingness, nor perception, nor non-perception, neither this world nor that world, nor sun, nor moon. And that, monks, there is no coming nor going, nor staying, nor passing, nor arising. It is unfixed, unmovable, without foundation. It is the end of suffering....

There is, monks, an unborn, uncreated, unmade, unformed. For if there was not that unborn, uncreated, unmade, unformed escape would not be possible from the born, created, made, formed. But since, monks, there is this unborn, uncreated, unmade, unformed, escape is possible from the born, created, made, formed."

Crossing to the Other Shore
[The Dhammapada]

6. The Wise Ones

85. There are few who reach the other shore. Most simply keep running up and down this shore.

86. But those who follow the *dhamma*, when it has been well taught, will reach the other shore, passing beyond the realm of death.

87. The wise ones leave darkness behind and follow the way of light. Going from their homes into the homeless state, they find their joy in renunciation, where others say it is hard to find.

88. Leaving all pleasures behind, and calling nothing their own, the wise ones free themselves from all the defilements of the mind.

89. Those who are well-grounded...who are freed from all clinging and attachments, whose appetites are conquered, and who are full of light—they have attained *Nibbāna* even in this very life.

Alt. Trans: DMP, p. 97, 195-199.

26. The Brahmin

383. Cross the stream valiantly, O Brahmin! Cut off all your passion. Knowing the end of what has been created, you will come to know that which is uncreated.

384. When the Brahmin has reached the other shore...then all his chains will fall away because of the knowledge he has acquired.

385. Him I call the Brahmin for whom there is neither this shore nor that shore nor both shores and who is free from all fear.

386. Him I call the Brahmin who is meditative, pure, calm, dutiful, free from passion, and who has attained the final goal.

387. The sun shines by day and the moon by night. The warrior shines in armor, the Brahmin in meditation. But the Buddha, the Awakened One, shines radiantly both day and night.

402. Him I call the Brahmin, who in this life knows the end of suffering, who has laid all his burdens aside, and is unshackled.

414. Him I call the Brahmin, who has traveled through the labyrinth of becoming and has crossed the stream, difficult to cross, reaching the other shore, who is meditative, calm, free from doubts and desires, and who has attained *Nibbāna*.

421. Him I call the Brahmin, who doesn't cling to anything in past, present or future, who is poor and is free of all attachments.

422. Him I call the Brahmin who is valiant, noble, and heroic, the great sage, the conqueror—the one who has accomplished the goal and who has become awakened.

423. Him I call the Brahmin who possesses knowledge of his former lives, who knows heaven and hell, who has reached the end of future becomings. Supreme in wisdom, he has accomplished all that is to be accomplished.

Borobudur Buddha (Java, Indonesia, 9th century)

APPENDIX I

Buddha by the Numbers

3

The Three Refuges

1. The Buddha
2. The Dhamma
3. The Sangha

The Three Unwholesome Roots of Mind

1. Greed
2. Hatred
3. Delusion

The Three Wholesome Roots of Mind:

1. Non-Greed (Generosity)
2. Non-Hatred (Love)
3. Non-Delusion (Wisdom)

4

The Four Divine Abodes:

1. Loving-Kindness
2. Compassion
3. Joy
4. Equanimity

The Four Noble Truths:

1. There is suffering.

2. There is a cause of suffering.
3. There is the cessation of suffering.
4. There is the path leading to the cessation of suffering: The Noble Eightfold Path.

The Four Foundations of Mindfulness

1. Mindfulness of the Body
2. Mindfulness of Sensations
3. Mindfulness of Mind-States
4. Mindfulness of Mind-Objects

5

The Five Hindrances

1. Sensual Desire
2. Aversion
3. Sloth and Drowsiness
4. Restlessness and Worry
5. Doubt

The Five Aggregates

1. Material Form
2. Sensations
3. Perception
4. Volition
5. Consciousness

8

The Noble Eightfold Path:

1. Right Understanding
2. Right Intention
3. Right Speech
4. Right Action
5. Right Livelihood
6. Right Effort
7. Right Mindfulness
8. Right Concentration

APPENDIX II

Glossary of Pali Terms

akusala: unwholesome, bad

anatta: non-self

anicca: impermanent

arahant: a worthy one; a fully liberated person

bhikkhu/bhikkhuni: Buddhist monk/nun

bhavana: mental development, meditation

Bodhisatta: a future Buddha. This is how the Buddha used to describe himself prior to his enlightenment.

brahmavihara: divine abode (i.e., loving kindness, compassion, joy, equanimity)

Buddha: a fully awakened being, an enlightened being

citta: mind, mind-heart

dhamma: the teachings of the Buddha, phenomena

dukkha: suffering, unsatisfactoriness

jhāna: state of absorption

kamma: volitional action, karma

kaya: material body

khandha: aggregate (i.e., material form, sensations, perception, mental formations, consciousness)

kilesas: defilements

kusala: wholesome, good

metta: loving-kindness

Nibbana: liberation, enlightenment, release from suffering (lit. "to become extinguished")

pañña: wisdom

parinibbana: final extinction, final liberation

samadhi: concentration

samatha: serenity, tranquility, calm-abiding

samma: right

sangha: Buddhist community

satipatthana: foundation of mindfulness

sila: morality

sukha: happiness, joy

sutta: text containing a teaching of the Buddha

tanha: craving (lit. "thirst")

Tathagata: "one who has thus gone" and "one who has thus come" (i.e., one who is beyond coming and going or who has attained enlightenment). This is the term that the Buddha most often uses to describe himself in the texts of the Pali Canon.

vedana: feeling, sensation

vipassana: insight

Sources

Primary Sources (Pali Canon)

AN   *Anguttara Nikaya* (The Numerical Discourses of the Buddha). Trans. Bhikkhu Bodhi. Somerville, MA: Wisdom Publications, 2012.

DMP   *The Dhammapada.* Trans. Eknath Easwaran. Tomales, CA: Nilgiri Press, 1985.

DN   *Digha Nikaya* (Long Discourses of the Buddha). Trans. Maurice Walsh. Somerville, MA: Wisdom Publications, 2012.

MN   *Mihhhima Nikaya* (The Middle Length Discourses of the Buddha). Trans. Bhikkhu Nanamoli and Bhikkhu Bodhi. Somerville, MA: Wisdom Publications, 2009.

SN   *Samyutta Nikaya* (The Connected Discourses of the Buddha). Trans. Bhikkhu Bodhi. Somerville, MA: Wisdom Publications, 2000.

UD   *The Udana and the Itivuttaka: Two Classics from the Pali Canon.* Trans. John D. Ireland. Kandy, Sri Lanka: Buddhist Publication Society, 1997.

V   *Vinaya Pitaka* (The Book of the Discipline). Vol. 4. *Mahāvagga.* Trans. I.B. Horner. London: Luzac and Co., 1962.

Secondary Sources

Anālayo. *Satipatthana: The Direct Path to Realization.* Cambridge: Windhorse Publications, 2003.

Anderson, Carol. *Pain and Its Ending: The Four Noble Truths in the Theravada Canon.* New York: Routledge, 1999.

Armstrong, Karen. *Buddha.* London: Orion, 2004.

Batchelor, Martine. *The Spirit of the Buddha.* New Haven: Yale University Press, 2010.

Batchelor, Stephen. *Buddhism Without Beliefs.* New York: Riverhead Books, 1997.

— . *Confessions of a Buddhist Atheist.* New York: Spiegel and Grau, 2010.

Brasington, Leigh. *Right Concentration: A Practical Guide to the Jhanas.* Boston, MA: Shambhala, 2015.

Bodhi, Bhikkhu. *The Noble Eightfold Path: The Way to the End of Suffering.* Onalaska, WA: Pariyatta Publishing, 1998.

Dalai Lama. *The Four Noble Truths.* London: Thorsons, 1998.

Gethin, Rupert. *The Foundations of Buddhism.* Oxford, UK: Oxford University Press, 1998.

Gunaratana, Henepola. *The Path of Serenity and Insight.* New Delhi: Motilal Banarsidass, 2009.

Hagen, Steve. *Buddhism is Not What You Think.* New York: HarperCollins, 2002.

Hanh, Tich Nhat. *The Heart of the Buddha's Teaching.* New York: Broadway Books, 1999.

Keown, Damien. *Buddhism: A Very Short Introduction.* Oxford, UK: Oxford University Press, 1996.

Lopez, Donald S. *The Story of Buddhism: A Concise Guide to Its History and Teachings.* New York: HarperCollins, 2001.

Mizuno, Kogen. *The Beginnings of Buddhism.* Tokyo: Kōsea Publishing Co., 1989.

Moffitt, Philip. *Dancing with Life: Buddhist Insights for Finding Meaning and Joy in the Face of Suffering.* New York: Rodale Books, 2008.

Nanamoli, Bhikkhu. *Life of the Buddha (According to the Pali*

Canon). Kandy, Sri Lanka: Buddhist Publication Society, 1972.

Rahula, Walpola. *What the Buddha Taught*. New York: Grove Press, 1974.

Ross, Nancy Wilson. *Buddhism: A Way of Life and Thought*. New York: Alfred A. Knopf, 1980.

Schumann, H.W. *The Historical Buddha: The Times, Life and Teachings of the Founder of Buddhism*. New York: Arkana, 1989.

Shankman, Richard. *The Experience of Samadhi*. Boston, MA: Shambhala, 2008.

Smith, Huston and Novak, Philip. *Buddhism: A Concise Introduction*. New York: HarperCollins, 2003.

Smith, Jean. *The Beginner's Guide to Walking the Buddha's Eightfold Path*. New York: Bell Tower, 2002.

Solé-Leris, Amadeo. *Tranquillity and Insight*. Kandy, Sri Lanka: Buddhist Publication Society, 1992.

Sucitto, Ajan. *Turning the Wheel of Truth: Commentary on the Buddha's First Teaching*. Boston MA: Shambhala, 2010.

Summedho, Ajahn. *The Mind and the Way: Buddhist Reflections on Life*. Boston: Wisdom Publications, 1995.

Surya Das, Lama. *Awakening the Buddha Within*. New York: Broadway Books, 1997.

Thera, Nyanaponika. *Satipatthana: The Heart of Buddhist Meditation*. Kandy, Sri Lanka: Buddhist Publication Society, 1962.

—. *The Buddha's Path to Deliverance*. Seattle WA: BPS Pariyatti Editions, 2010.

Thomas, Edward J. *The Life of Buddha: As Legend and History*. New York: Routledge, 1996.

Made in USA - Kendallville, IN
1220212_9781539858737
12.30.2020 1025